GREAT BATTLES OF THE GREAT WAR

Other books by Michael Stedman

Salford Pals: *Pals Series*
Manchester Pals: *Pals Series*
Thiepval: *Battleground Europe Series*
La Boisselle: *Battleground Europe Series*
Fricourt-Mametz: *Battleground Europe Series*
Guillemont: *Battleground Europe Series*

MICHAEL STEDMAN
ED SKELDING

GREAT BATTLES
of the
GREAT WAR

Accompanies the major ITV series

Leo Cooper

First published in 1999 by
LEO COOPER
an imprint of
Pen & Sword Books Ltd
47 Church Street
Barnsley
South Yorkshire
S70 2AS

A CIP catalogue record for this book is available from the British Library

ISBN 0 85052 702 3

Printed in Great Britain by The Bath Press

INTRODUCTION

The Writer's perspective

A friend recently reminded me that people who make no study of history are doomed to repeat it. That phrase encapsulates one of the great conundrums of history. All too often we echo its bleakest passages with willing replication.

The Balkans, more than any other place in the last one thousand years, have come to illustrate that quandary of repetition better than most. The first, 11th century, European Crusaders passed this way en route to their appointment with mayhem in the Holy Land. The slaughter of Muslim innocents by Christian pilgrims and soldiers who survived that first terrible journey to the prize of Jerusalem has set the subsequent schedule of the Balkans in this meeting place of religious intolerance. This inhospitable corner of south-eastern Europe maintains many deeply ingrained sentiments, many of which are consequential upon the Turkish Ottoman Empire's control of parts of the Balkans, Asia and North Africa between the late 13th and early 20th centuries. These predilections still drive many agendas here to this day. It is therefore quite respectable to argue that the North Atlantic Treaty Organisation's confrontation with ethnic intolerance in Kosovo, here in the epicentre of the Balkans, has its roots in almost a thousand years of religious tension.

Yet we all know that there is nothing romantic about war. There wasn't in the 11th century and there isn't today.

There is no point in ascribing gentle interpretation to the history of war. As one character within a remarkable novel which describes the soldiers' experience of the Great War said, 'There's too much f...in' artillery in this bloody war...You don't get no sleep.'[1] Such grumbling, stoical humour was

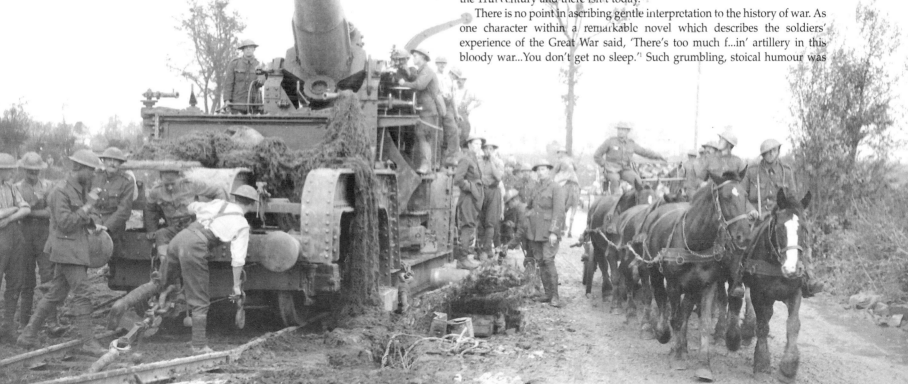

the hallmark of the British Tommy, and he was all the better for it. But at the less humorous end of the Great War's documentation let me mention the minutes of a military conference held during the middle period of the Battle for Passchendaele. Within the ghastly and inhuman prevailing conditions the soldiers were encouraged forward, during assaults, behind a protective barrage of shells. The indescribable ferocity of that curtain of hellish detonations can only be imagined. Yet as the conference revealed - 'The only means of knowing whether troops are sufficiently close to the barrage is when casualties are inflicted by our own artillery.'[2]

This wasn't an accidental occurrence of that meaningless late 20th century phrase 'friendly fire'. It was the certainty of casualties 'inflicted by our own artillery'. That indeed was a very hard lesson to learn.

A glance through the imagery which dominates these pages will help you understand the purpose of this book. It is not a guide-book or travelogue. Nor is it a source of detail in the form of a reference work. What I hope this text and the illustrations provide is a fresh and evocative look at the imagery of the Great War. Clearly it would be foolish to suggest that by reading and viewing the following pages you will have understood the enormous complexity of the Great War. After thirty years of interest and study I would never claim to have fully comprehended all it has to offer. I simply know a little about a small fragment of what happened. However, what I do know for certain is that those four years which ground a grotesque path through the early years of the 20th Century's history have marked and defined some of the worst fears of man. They were one of the lowest points in a century repeatedly characterised by the pointless slaughter of thousands, sometimes millions, of humans. In response to the ugly brutality of the First World War historians and commentators have generated an enormous body of analytic and descriptive literature. This book is not intended to add to that imponderable quantity of words.

Just one history lesson!

The catalyst of the Great War was death in Sarajevo on 28 June, 1914. The Balkan states, Greece, Albania, Serbia and others, were then, as now, the focus of both western and Russian concern as the gradual collapse of Turkish control left opportunities for Balkan states to argue amongst themselves. Since the late 13th century Turkey had maintained the vast Ottoman Empire by rule from Constantinople, although by 1914 they were not masters of that

disparate and far-flung collection of peoples. Two years earlier, in 1912, the Balkan League, comprising Serbia, Montenegro, Bulgaria and Greece, had declared war on Turkey, effectively ending Turkish influence in the area. The following year, 1913, the Balkan pot had overheated again as Serbia and Bulgaria bickered over the territories lost by the Ottoman Empire's crumbling. Serbia's victory and the sentiment of her strong ethnic links with Russia meant that she became a threat to the stability of the Austro-Hungarian Empire.

There had already been one Bosnian crisis, during 1909, when Russia had failed Serbia and allowed the annexation of this region by the Austro-Hungarians. When the heir to the throne of that empire, Archduke Franz Ferdinand, was assassinated by Gavrilo Princep, a Serbian nationalist, in Sarajevo on 28 June, that single event unleashed the forces of the Great War. An ultimatum was issued to Serbia but its terms were deemed unacceptable. However, Germany's alliance with Austro-Hungary enabled the former to be persuaded of the need to provide support. The Austro-Hungarians were encouraged and declared war on the Serbians. Russia responded in kind with a declaration of war upon Austria-Hungary. This brought forth the involvement of France, Russia's ally, and Germany. Britain, though not bound by the terms of any alliance, was soon brought into the conflict when German troops invaded Belgium as part of their plan to defeat the French. Britain, as a guarantor of Belgian neutrality, was incorporated.

The Great War was fact. It was 11.00 pm on 4 August 1914.

Eighty-five years later it seems incredible that, as the 20th century flows into a new millennium, Turkey, Serbia and the explosive ethnic and religious contrasts which mark this part of the world astride the Bosphorus, scene of the ill-fated Gallipoli campaign, are still the focus of our fears.

Within the terrible journey through the slough of despondency which the four years of the Great War became there were many significant battles in what became a global conflict. John Bourne has pointed up the statistics lucidly:

'There are some who dispute the status of the Great War as a 'true' World War. This is perverse. The conflict was global. Major wars were fought not only in western, eastern and southern Europe, but also in the Middle East and the Caucasus. A lesser - guerrilla - war tied down more than 100,000 British Empire troops in East Africa. Surface fleets and submarines contested naval supremacy on and under the oceans of the world. But this was far from all. The insatiable demands of war

1. Frederick Manning. *The Middle Parts of Fortune*, Peter Davies, 1977.

2. 62nd Infantry Brigade, 29/30th September 1917. Quoted in *Passchendaele in Perspective*. Ed. Liddle. Leo Cooper/Pen and Sword Books Ltd, 1997.

3. *Passchendaele in Perspective*, Ed., P.Liddle, Leo Cooper/Pen & Sword, 1997.

extended far beyond the battlefields, not least because two of the major belligerents, Great Britain and France, were imperial powers with access to global resources of manpower, raw materials and food. The 'British' Army eventually recruited 1.6 million Indians, 630,000 Canadians, 412,000 Australians, 136,000 South Africans, 130,000 New Zealanders and approximately 50,000 Africans, as well as several hundred thousand Chinese 'coolies'. The 'French' Army recruited 600,000 North and West Africans as combat troops and a further 200,000 as labourers. The ability of the Entente to command the manpower and natural resources of Africa, Asia, Australasia and North and South America made a major contribution to victory. The political and economic impact of this global mobilisation was also immense.'[3]

The consequences were vast and far-reaching for all the corners of the globe. By the war's end Russia had been plunged into the Bolshevik revolution as a direct consequence of the conflict's impact upon her society. The United States of America had been drawn into the European mêlée by Germany's ill-advised use of unrestricted submarine warfare. The British Empire was fatally wounded. European monarchies were swept away. Boundaries too numerous to contemplate were about to be changed with far-reaching consequences for nations, ethnic groupings and future generations.

So why choose these three battles?

The answer is a simple one. Gallipoli, the Somme and Passchendaele were all launched as offensive battles by the British armed forces in the anticipation of affecting both the course and outcome of the war. Their progenitors and planners had great expectations. The outcome of each battle was, however, in each case unexpected. All three added significantly to the growing catalogue of misery which the Great War spawned. All three generated enduring imagery whose hold on our society's collective memory is still powerful: debilitating hardship, disease and the omnipresent flies which settled eagerly upon every meagre mouthful of food in the heat of Gallipoli, stoical lines of disciplined volunteers marching forward, their rifles shouldered; part of every sad reflection on the futility of the Somme campaign's tragic opening. The hideous circumstances of soldiers sucked into the mud's enveloping foulness on the slopes beneath Passchendaele village. It is not surprising that all three have come to be regarded, in popular interpretation, as British failures. That interpretation is, however, not a correct one.

The images within this book can only be a stepping stone. Across the flood of detailed words which is still written about the Great War the following pages denote a series of places which should be burnished into our collective memory. The tranquillity and languid peace which marks their atmosphere today is in utter contrast to the loathsome reality which once unfolded there.

Viewing Ed Skelding's remarkable documentary history of these three great struggles is both a harrowing and uplifting experience. The programmes are compelling because of the unique juxtaposition of bleak contemporary footage with the captivating colour and textures which abound in those same locations today. To stand and witness the rows upon desolate rows of graves shimmering in the heat of the Turkish sun, to see the bright

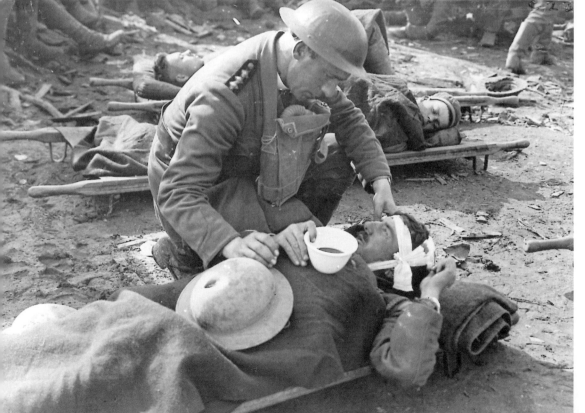

faces of volunteer soldiers riding the flood of expectant optimism before the Somme nightmare unfolded, to see the footage of battle-weary soldiers dragging the very vestiges of their last energy across the sodden battlefields of Flanders is to understand. Look carefully at each programme as its images move across your television's screen. This was the first war where reality was captured on film, where photographers and artists looked into the eyes of men at war and saw the terror that we all pray we never have to meet with.

My intent:

'Less is best' is the maxim by which this volume has been created.

The book is intended, unashamedly, to be atmospheric. My intention is to reveal something of the legacy which these great battles have left in situ. There is a sense of history, something which I call the *cathedral experience*, when you stand within such battlefields. I have seen adults and children alike weep at the understanding of Thiepval's stark truth. The very utterance of Passchendaele's strangely haunting name is enough to stop any correctly prepared school group in its track. To look across the solidly agrarian scene towards Tyne Cot cemetery's vivid architecture, which rises shockingly within the surrounding calm, is to understand at once the cost of war. By contrast with the human forfeit endured within the 1917 battles for Passchendaele the campaigning on Gallipoli in 1915 produced a light harvest for the grim reaper. Yet Gallipoli's harsh circumstance were, in so many ways, the birthplace of Australian self-consciousness – born of the hideous circumstances of her wounded and maimed soldiers' evacuation from those evil hillsides. It would be inappropriate to describe Gallipoli as anything other than a 'Great Battle of the Great War', even though its battle casualties, spread over eight months, amounted to a total rather less than those experienced elsewhere during the grim years of 1916 and 1917.

These three Great Battles have been the subject of millions of words. Some accounts are academic and arid; others are inspiringly readable. Thousands of small works were published immediately after the war, describing a unit's contribution to the war effort, sometimes official, sometimes a casual and comradely testimony of shared hardships, anguish and loss. Latterly many histories have drawn, quite rightly, upon the fund of personal reminiscences which were recorded in great number towards the end of the participants' long lives[4]. Yet the text you will find on the subsequent pages can be read within an evening. Each chapter is formed from a brief explanation of why the battle was significant and how it came to be undertaken. Therefore, this book is not intended to be read as a definitive or chronological history. Its purpose is to provide a focal point of empathy. Not a reference work, but something to remind your heart why we need to know and why we shouldn't forget.

Opposite each of Ed Skelding's powerful images you will find my running commentary or explanation, as well as a caption explaining a little of the photograph's background and context. Many of Ed's photographs, taken with such care during the last three years, have an ethereal quality. The space and depth within each provide the chance to ponder how evil could have left such a mesmerically attractive legacy. Within the commentary and explanation I have made use of a number of sources and devices:

◆ Illustrative extracts from Official History sources[5].
◆ Extracts from other contemporary printed materials[6] including personal accounts and diary extracts.
◆ Brief extracts from military unit records such as Divisional, Brigade or Battalion diaries.
◆ A map of the action or a map of the area/theatre of war.

◆ A contemporary image or photograph of the participants and locations. These might be atmospheric images of soldiers and personalities or the terrible consequences of war, its unthinking death and destruction.

The extraordinary thing about the Great War is that its many layers can be peeled back as if by an archaeologist. Each layer is met by doubt that so many were involved, that so much was lost. Each look deeper into the history and its fascinating wealth of anecdote, detail, tragedy, inspiration and humanity is almost invariably accompanied by a period of reflection and self-appraisal, sometimes simply by a sense of sadness or even tears.

Your discovery of a little fragment of history, perhaps a walk where your antecedents fought, maybe a single charge case from a spent round plucked from the battlefield, a photograph in a rusty box in the attic, all invariably lead to a desire to find out more.

It is my hope that you will be able to return in person to each and all of these places. In their own ways every one will both haunt and reward your journeying to meet with their peculiar and transfixing ambience. It is as if by being there, in places which have been traumatised and raped by the very worst which the 20th century has done, that we as individuals can be renewed. These places provide opportunities to learn of our frailty, of our own strengths and the reasons why we should deploy that strength with caution, concern and liberality. When utilised by skilled teachers, the Somme is one of the greatest classrooms, a learning experience without equal. There I have seen some of the finest lessons driven home to enraptured students by teachers whose skill is enhanced and honed by being within this incredible environment. And those lessons have nothing to do with the promotion of nationalism or looking insensitively backwards in the belief that the men who fought the war were in some way a 'lost and finer generation'. These places are full of the most important messages and lessons for young people today. They should be visited and learned from. We are all the better for doing so.

If you haven't yet been, to some or all of these places, I can only counsel that you should. If you have, and are familiar with the places pictured within this book, I can only hope that its imagery is both evocative and meaningful.

Michael Stedman, *Leigh, Worcestershire. May 1999.*

---

4. The Department of Sound Records in the Imperial War Museum holds an intriguing, informative and evocative collection of superb recordings detailing every aspect of service and life during the Great War.

5. *Military Operations. France and Belgium.* Also: *Military Operations. Gallipoli.* The many volumes of the Official British History of the Great War are usually available in the larger reference libraries. Facsimile copies are, in the case of many of the volumes, available from the Imperial War Museum in London.

6. Many units, though by no means all, which participated during the Great War were, afterwards, drawn into the production of a unit history which recounted the service of that Battalion, Brigade or Division. Some serving soldiers and groups also produced their memoirs. The process of publication of such materials including diaries and letters goes on to this day. The diaries on which these histories are based can be found in the Public Record Office.

The Photographer's Perspective

Of all the twentieth century's grim wars, the First World War stands out as a particularly tragic event. Many hundreds of thousands of men marched off to their deaths in a series of desperate battles that would ultimately become known as the Great War. It was great in terms of the number of nations involved, in the number of places across the world where the battles took place, but most of all it is remembered for the great number who were killed.

More than ten million people died, most of them on battlefields whose names became part of everyday conversation during the war years of 1914 to 1918: places like Mons and Loos and Vimy Ridge. But there were three that emerged as the most dreaded: Gallipoli, the Somme and Passchendaele. All three had particularly tragic twists that added both to their evil reputations and to the death tolls, giving them a special place in the public memory.

In recent years interest in the Great War has risen steadily, growing beyond that of the military enthusiast or of the groups and institutions dedicated to preserving its memory. As awareness of many of the more tragic aspects of the war grows, so does the number of people visiting the battlefields for the first time.

To help in furthering that awareness, I have spent much of the past six years producing a series of television documentaries covering the course of those three great battles, now with the collective title Great Battles of the Great War. Over the years of filming it became clear that this was the only title that could do justice to the subjects of the endeavour.

Prior to filming the often complex and disjointed chain of events that make up a battle, it was essential to undertake a visit to each of the locations, to see for myself the place where key actions took place. On each of these occasions the impact the battlefield had on me was a powerful one. Visiting the Somme for the first time was a memorable experience. The endless rows of headstones in the carefully maintained cemeteries, the striking landscape still bearing the scars of the conflict, the many monuments and relics together conjured up an unforgettable image of the battlefield.

It was summer when I first visited the Gallipoli Peninsula. It was hot, with blue skies and sun-bleached sand. Walking this battlefield was an often stunning experience, standing on the spot where many vital actions were played out. It is a feature of the Gallipoli battlefield that each of the three main areas at Helles, Anzac and Suvla cover a comparatively small area of gound, testimony to just how tenuous a grip the Allies held on the peninsula.

What was even more astounding was the fact that in 1994, the year before my first visit, the thick forest of pine trees that covered the Anzac area as part of the national park had been almost completely burnt off the ridges and gullies by a spectacular forest fire. This after a luckless shepherd boy had set fire to the tinder-dry bush while cooking a meal.

The result was that virtually the entire area of Anzac and the Sari Bair Ridge was cleared of trees. In just a few days, the battlefield was again fully visible for the first time in eighty years. It would be another year before we returned to film it, and though the vegetation was rapidly regaining control, the images we obtained are quite unique.

Ypres is perhaps the most difficult of the three battlefields to film. Unlike the open and largely unchanged landscape of the Somme and Gallipoli, Ypres is a city surrounded by a close-knit network of smaller towns and villages. The land here is constantly farmed, with a network of new roads and new building developments. Yet it would be impossible to come to the century's greatest killing ground and not find ample evidence of the ultimate horror that was The Salient.

Four years of relentless struggle saw this place emerge as the most sinister of the lot. While Gallipoli had the romance of a foreign crusade and the Somme the sad legacy of doomed youth, the name Ypres was destined to be remembered for the mud and squalor and the degradation of human life. The memorials are here, so too are a great number of concrete blockhouses, mine craters and even trenches. Ypres is a challenging battlefied to know and understand. So much happened here after four years of war, that it takes much research and some good guides to get near to understanding the series of events that would ultimately lead to Passchendaele.

On each of these reconnaissance trips I have taken my stills cameras to help record particular locations, this with the intention of returning to the same spot with the film crew. All of these photographs were taken using hand-held Nikon 35mm cameras. It is very much in the nature of walking the battlefields that this format of camera is particularly apt for the job. Often the objective is to cover a lot of ground, so the less kit the better. It also offers the opportunity to react to the shot as it presents itself, given that much research has gone into specific locations and the time of day. As much as possible, the reader has been put on the spot where they might experience the same view as a soldier at the time.

That in essence, is the reason for this book. These photographs are part of the original framework that went into the construction of these programmes.

To that extent, many of the images in this book will strike a chord with any who have seen the programmes.

I am delighted to have had the opportunity of collaborating with Michael Stedman in the preparation and development of this book. I have admired his particular style of writing about the Great War through his contributions to the Battleground Europe series and looked forward to our first meeting. We agreed that the motivation and direction for this book should be to make it different from others about the Great War. While hundreds of text books are available detailing every move and possible strategy, there were none that concentrated on the photography in a way that might show how these battlefields look now. I hope that by making this book accessible to those who know little or nothing about the Great War, it will prompt a visit to one or more of these fascinating places.

My thanks to my daughter Louise Tindill and Ward Philpson Photolabs for their assistance in helping compile these prints. Thanks also to the many who have helped in the making of the television series, but above all to my wife Margaret who has helped me through some very difficult times during the past six years.

Ed Skelding, Newcastle upon Tyne May 1999

CHAPTER ONE

GALLIPOLI
The Last Crusade

Ten years before the Great War the ailing ramshackle administration of Turkey stood at the head of a once vast sovereignty, the Ottoman Empire. In its heyday that empire's administration had controlled much of Asia Minor, Greece and the Mediterranean. By the early years of this century a sequence of wars had so weakened her authority that Turkey was known disdainfully as 'the sick man of Europe'. Nevertheless, loose Turkish control still stretched across the eastern Mediterranean, part of the North African coast, the European Balkans to the Adriatic sea and north-eastwards to Russia. However, accelerating political and economic disintegration turned the restive and reluctant outposts of the Ottoman Empire into attractive targets for European powers seeking to extend their influence at this crucial juncture of east and west, between Muslim and Orthodox Christian traditions and culture.

Into this opportunity strode the Young Turks whose political leader was the bleakly cruel Talaat Bey. By direct and malicious means these men challenged every example of inertia in the old empire's creaking structures. They were ruthless in the pursuit of power and in their determination to wield that power. The country's autocratic and repressive ruler of more than thirty years, Sultan Abdul Hamid II or 'Abdul the Damned', was overthrown by the Young Turks in 1909 and replaced by his younger brother, the dynamically moribund Mohammed V. Mohammed was destined to be a front, a figurehead, utterly deferential to the Young Turks. They restored the more liberal constitution which had been removed by Abdul Hamid in 1877 but the reality was that a new totalitarianism had been established. The Young Turks' background and brutal methods were utterly incongruent with the restrained manners which identified other early 20th century European politicians and diplomats.

Any pretence at democracy was quickly cast aside. The Empire's administration remained chaotic. During the Balkan Wars of 1912-13 Turkey was sent spinning to a predictably crushing defeat by Bulgaria, Serbia, Greece and Montenegro. She was open to both threats and appeals from Germany and Russia, from her Balkan opponents such as Bulgaria and Greece, from France and, to a lesser extent, Britain.

In this context 1915's events upon the sun-bleached slopes of the Gallipoli peninsula have their origins in a long-standing British interest in the Dardanelles. Prior to the outbreak of war the British General Staff and the Admiralty had considered contingency plans concerned with the possibility of forcing this narrow strip of water, in the event that military and strategic circumstances dictated such a course of action. The most recent study, in 1911,

The Dardanelles - the view to Chanak and The Narrows. (opposite)
This photograph was taken on the eastern side of the peninsula which was within the area controlled by French troops. Travelling to the higher ground of the Sari Bair Ridge and its central feature, Chunuk Bair, you can observe an extraordinary and improbable view across these waters. That high ground was what the ANZACs coveted and which they came so close to capturing. From there you can see the Aegean islands of Imbros and Samothrace. Away to the south west across the Dardanelles, in Turkey, you can see the Trojan plain and Mount Ida beyond. Europe and Asia in one moment. Yet all this is visible from a vantage point just 850 feet in altitude!

The Dardanelles seem little more substantial than a stretch of the River Severn or Thames as they near their estuaries. However, these waters are a unique feature in the world's nautical topography. They connect the Mediterranean Sea with the Sea of Marmara and thus the Black Sea. This is therefore Russia's Mediterranean access and it is the defining location between European culture's influence and the Middle East.

These turbulent waters are never still. There is a ceaseless traffic of ferries, oil tankers, cargo and military vessels here. The Dardanelles are just over 40 miles in length. Their exit, between Sedd-el-Bahr and Kum Kale, is just 4,000 yards wide. As you progress eastwards into the Dardanelles the banks widen to more than four miles but at the Narrows between Chanak Kale and Kilid Bahr those banks close to within 1,600 yards before subsequently widening again en route for the Sea of Marmara. As with all Mediterranean waters there is little or no tide to speak of, but throughout the seasons a current of some four to five knots flows south westwards, carrying water from the Black Sea rivers to the open seas.

had concluded that it was not feasible 'to force the Dardanelles'.

However, Britain failed to hold fast to that lesson and was soon drawn, during the months before the outbreak of war, into an atmosphere of bad blood between herself and Turkey. That atmosphere was fuelled by one of the brigands who formed the Turkish government in 1914, the handsome, dynamic and strongly pro-German Enver Pasha, Minister of War. Perversely Turkey had, in 1910, sought an alliance with Britain when Enver Pasha had

met and impressed Churchill. That fleeting chance of ensuring Turkish neutrality in any forthcoming conflict was ultimately squandered so that, by late 1914, Britain was attracted by the chances of effectively deploying her great naval strength against Europe's sick man. The varied coastlines of the seemingly decrepit and crumbling Ottoman Empire were immensely lengthy – indefensibly so. Our ambassador in Constantinople, Sir Louis Mallet, believed that The Narrows were capable of being forced by a determined naval assault. His views were influential upon Churchill whose position within the British Cabinet, since 1911, was as First Lord of the Admiralty.

The weeks before the declaration of war between Britain and Germany, rather belatedly on 5 November 1914, were to give Enver Pasha every opportunity to exercise his pro-German feelings. In 1911 and again in 1913 the Turkish Government had ordered battleships from British shipyards. Public subscriptions within Turkey, fuelled by patriotic fervour, had raised the money. Powerful UK shipbuilding companies, including the Armstrong company at Elswick on Tyneside, offered to build the necessary facilities, reaching agreement with the Turks in December of 1913. The ships, *Sultan Osman I* and the *Reshadieh* were ready to sail to Turkey by the end of July 1914.

Troy. *(opposite)*
This is a stunning vantage point from which to overlook a 20th century battlefield. What history and controversy this place has witnessed. The dazzling site of Troy lies no more than five miles from the Aegean Sea, overlooking the Dardanelles. Underneath the mound at Hissarlik – 'The Place of Fortresses' – the German archaeologist Henrich Schliemann, working here in 1870, found the remains of nine phases of occupation, ending in the Roman era, thereby spanning the greatest part of pre-Christian history in the eastern Mediterranean. This place was the focus of the Trojan War, fought here three millennia ago, described in epic poems by Homer. The ancient Greeks knew this place as Ilium, after its founding figure, Ilus, the son of Tros.

Looking to the Aegean Sea from Troy is to look across the site of the French landings at Kum Kale on the Turkish mainland on the morning of 25 April 1915.

Many regarded the name 'Troy' as a figment of legend, but Schliemann, guided by Homer's Iliad, undertook the excavations which revealed stone walls and the battlements of an ancient city at Hissarlik. Some of Schliemann's discoveries were of spectacular importance including the cache of gold, bronze, and silver objects known as Priam's Treasure, taken from the Troy III levels.

Initially those treasures were displayed in Athens but were soon sent to Berlin where they stayed until the end of the Second World War. In 1993 the treasures were again revealed at the Pushkin museum in Moscow and the Hermitage museum in St. Petersburg. Controversy still rages over the ownership of these Bronze Age artefacts, persuasive claims being made by Turkey, Greece, Germany and Russia!

Five hundred Turkish sailors arrived on Tyneside to man the *Sultan Osman I* and prepare for her removal to Turkish waters.

The more powerful of these two ships, *Reshadieh*, was a modern and potentially dangerous adversary: a Super Dreadnought of 23,000 tons, capable of 21 knots, with a primary armament of ten 13.5 inch guns. Those huge weapons were capable of launching a 14,800 lb. broadside, superior to that of any British vessel. Even the *Sultan Osman* was a formidably well-armed vessel with fourteen 12 inch guns capable of launching a broadside of 12,900 lb. The Admiralty and Churchill were uncertain of the merits of this transfer of naval power, especially to a state whose neutrality was not guaranteed. On 1st August Britain commandeered the Turkish vessels offering financial compensation to soften the blow. Enver Pasha wouldn't

The ruins of the fort at Sedd-el-Bahr. (above and opposite)
The twin fortresses at Sedd-el-Bahr and Kum Kale define the outer limits of the Dardanelles. Initial attacks here on 3 November 1914 did limited damage to the forts' structures but it was the crushing weight of naval shells fired on 19 February 1915 which wreaked such havoc inside the forts. By the time The Narrows were due to be forced on 18 March the forts at Sedd-el-Bahr and Kum Kale were reduced to feebleness in preventing entry into the Dardanelles. However, the fort at Sedd-el-Bahr subsequently witnessed the landings at V beach at close quarters. The small spit of rock against which the River Clyde *was beached is still here. Today it is frequented by holidaymakers, sunbathers and swimmers looking for a secure foothold in the warm Aegean waters.*

deal. The Turks were devastated, and regarded the acquisition as an act of theft.

Whilst British relations with Turkey plumbed the depths German influence became more significant. On 2 August 1914 Enver signed a secret alliance treaty which confirmed it completely, while Germany promised support in the event of a Russo-Turkish war. Although the British government was unaware of these events, the negotiations between Turkey and Germany were progressed whilst the British Government was deciding what to do with the *Sultan Osman* and the *Reshadieh*. In the circumstances the two ships were added to the Royal Navy's fleet complement with the new names *Agincourt* and *Erin*[1]. On 10 August the Turks further antagonised the British. On that date Turkey gave permission for the *Goeben* and *Breslau* to pass through the Dardanelles having escaped from the British Mediterranean Fleet. The following day, 11 August, the two German ships arrived at Constantinople, were bought by Turkey and renamed *Jawuz Sultan Selim* and *Midilli*. The German crews remained on board. The two ships would soon cause much difficulty and damage to Russian dignity in the Black Sea. Churchill, as First Lord of the Admiralty, was perpetually uneasy about this turn of events. It was his influence, in turn a reflection of Mallet's belief that The Narrows could be forced, which sparked the Gallipoli land forces' campaign of 1915.

---

1. After the war and following the Turkish surrender of 30 October 1918 these vessels stayed within the Royal Navy, becoming the only British battleships whose expense was borne by a foreign belligerent state!

That disjointed and ultimately futile crusade commenced in April 1915 when the Great War between the major European combatants was just eight months old. The greater part of the British regular army had already been decimated in the great defensive battles, of October and November 1914 to secure the town of Ypres in Belgium. Their successors were about to be thrust into a second battle of Ypres, one where chlorine gas would be deployed by the German army – the first use of indiscriminate chemical warfare on a massive scale.

In the context of wars which had already beset the planet this conflict was, as yet, an infant. But what had already marked the hostility as distinctive was the geographic and mechanical stalemate which had now been reached in the trench warfare of France and Flanders. From Switzerland to the North Sea a complex of trenches had already evolved. The attempts of each combatant to outflank each other on the Western Front during the autumn of 1914 had failed. Now, within that stalemate, the full brutal mechanisms of industrial power could be freely deployed through increasingly sophisticated and impersonal forms of weaponry.

Once Turkey became a belligerent on the side of the Central Powers, on 29 October 1914, the way was clearly open for Britain to deploy her traditional strength of naval power. In the European theatre of war, because of the very limited length of German coastline and the inaccessibility of the Baltic parts of that coastline, it had been difficult to visualise any seaborne assault on Germany being successful. But Turkey's extensive coastline seemed far more promising and susceptible to British naval strength. Britain declared war on

Turkey on 5 November. At the time few voices were raised to point out the great size of Turkish land forces, some 500,000 men with another 250,000 in reserve depots.

However, within the sterile and immobile European context the chosen tactics which unfolded on the Gallipoli peninsula were, potentially, both innovative and imaginative. Those operations would evolve into a combined naval and land forces operation against the Gallipoli peninsula, a narrow strip of land above the Dardanelles whose waters run between Asia and Europe. That chasm between culture and expectation had always been an uneasy one. Now, in April 1915, it was to escalate into an extraordinary battle whose purpose, seen from the British perspective, was to sever the influence of the Turks from the German - Austrian Central Powers.

This would be an outflanking manoeuvre on the grand scale.

The strategic importance of the Gallipoli peninsula's coast was clearly not lost on the German command. Any failure on Turkey's part to dominate The Narrows would then allow the British High Seas Fleet the opportunity to attempt to force a passage through the Bosphorus[2]. That severance would allow Russia access to the Mediterranean and enable, if not the opening then at least the real threat of, a third front in the land battle against the Central Powers.

Because of the area's clear and significant importance and the close links between the Turks and the Central Powers a German military advisory team had been established on Turkish soil since the early weeks of 1914. The mission had been requested by the Young Turks in 1913. That assignment, ostensibly to modernise the Ottoman Army, was ably led by General Liman von Sanders who was appointed Commander-in-Chief of the Turkish First Army on 27 August 1914. Prior to that a steady stream of German technicians, officers, instructors and war materiel had arrived during the first months of 1914 to revitalise the morale and efficiency of Turkey's army. Sanders' guidance had overseen the construction and development of limited defences along the Gallipoli peninsula's coastline. He had completely reorganised the tactics and training of Turkish infantry, turning men whose units had been unpaid and untrained into a dedicated and effective force.

In the context of this growing hostility Britain possessed a surfeit of ageing battleships whose guns and armour, though not up to the most modern naval requirements, would be able to sustain the sort of serious bombardment required to destroy the forts which dominated the entrance to the Dardanelles[3]. A preliminary to that bombardment had begun, with little idea of purpose, on 3 November 1914, and quite remarkably two days before Britain's declaration of war on Turkey. That day an Allied British and French squadron carried out a successful action against the outer Dardanelles forts, one of which suffered considerable damage when a shell penetrated the fort's magazine. There was nothing by way of reply from the Turks. However, the impact of that success was then allowed to evaporate.

December 1914 saw a suicidal attack on Russia, across the Caucasus, by ill-equipped Turkish troops. Almost 100,000 men in summer equipment were decimated as early as mid-January 1915, both by the barbarous weather and Russian counter-attack. However, this Turkish attempt to wage war on the Russians had far-reaching effects. The Russians requested support from Britain in the form of 'a demonstration of some kind against Turks elsewhere, either naval or military.' Even before that request had been made Lieutenant Holbrook in his submarine, B11, succeeded in penetrating the Turkish minefields before sinking an old warship, the *Messudieh*, in Sari Sighlar Bay on Sunday, 13 December.

The tone of Britain's response was set. Sea power would be used to defeat Turkey's alliance with the Central Powers.

In the early weeks of 1915 there seemed little prospect of a troop landing on Gallipoli. As early as 2 January Kitchener was telling Churchill that no men were available. A week later Admiral Carden, commanding the British

The **Nousret** *at Chanak naval base. (opposite)*
This is a symbol of great import to the Turkish people. It is difficult to underestimate its significance for Turkish visitors. It is the vessel from whose decks sprang the opportunity to defeat the Allied navies in 1915. That defeat is regarded as a fulcrum in the evolution of Turkey's twentieth century consciousness.
Today the mines and their laying equipment seem part of a quite innocent, almost innocuous, military technology. But the vessel's diminutive size and the simplicity of its purpose were the reasons why it was so successful. Eighty years on, in an era when individual battlefield soldiers deploy powerful weaponry at will, launching shoulder-held anti-tank missiles and summoning the support of precision artillery capable of firing accurately over vast range, when unseen submarines send forth missiles with devastating exactness, when warplanes travel habitually at more than the speed of sound and when leviathan battleships are a thing of the past, it is easy to miss the significance of this tiny vessel in Turkey's progress from being regarded as 'the sick man of Europe' to membership of NATO and aspirant European economy. That progress has never been simple or unruffled yet the Nousret, *perhaps better than any other piece of preserved battlefield technology or monumental memorial on the Gallipoli peninsula, epitomises that step forward into modernity.*

---

2. The Bosphorus is an even narrower stretch of water running between the Black Sea and the Sea of Marmara to the east of the Dardanelles. Istanbul (Constantinople) lies at the southern end of the Bosphorus.

3. As well as the *Queen Elizabeth*, Britain's most modern battleship of the era, carrying eight 15 inch guns, broadside 16,000 lbs., and capable of 25 knots.

East Mediterranean squadron, advised that the forts guarding The Narrows were open to a naval attack. Initially, on 28 January, the War Council in Britain would give approval only for a limited assault on the Gallipoli peninsula based on a naval bombardment. The plan, instigated by Churchill and Admiral Fisher, was for a fleet of old and expendable Dreadnought battleships to force the Dardanelles behind a gradual reduction of the forts by naval gunfire. Fisher was also concerned that, whilst the ships were dispensable, their crews most definitely were not. This situation played directly into the hands of the Turkish defences which were now far more dependent upon modern mobile artillery, rather than antiquated and vulnerable static forts. That artillery had a perfect adjunct in the policy of laying sequences of mines across the Dardanelles.

The Turkish defences were layered into three distinct zones:

• The Narrows. Less than a mile wide at their narrowest point between Chanak Kale, on the Turkish mainland, and Kilid Bahr, on the coast of the peninsula. Here a series of inner defences comprised eleven forts housing heavy guns as well as supporting mobile (howitzer) artillery hidden in the surrounding gullies and slopes. Spread across the narrows were five lines of anti-shipping mines all of which were capable of penetrating the hulls of Dreadnought battleships. If these narrows could be successfully crossed by Carden's vessels the way to Constantinople and the seat of Turkish government would be wide open through the Sea of Marmara.

• An intermediate zone again utilising mines laid in five lines stretching across the waters northwards from Kephez Point on the Turkish mainland. Again mobile howitzers were deployed with fields of fire covering the minefields which were illuminated at night by the sweeping beams of powerful searchlights.

• The outer defences covered the waters between Helles Point and Kum Kale. These were the most susceptible to naval bombardment since battleships could manoeuvre unhindered by mines in the more open waters of the Aegean Sea to the west of Sedd-el-Bahr fort, at Helles, and the Kum Kale fort.

Early February saw the introduction of a charismatic figure into this theatre of operations, the powerful and enigmatic Mustafa Kemal. On 2 February Kemal was appointed by Liman von Sanders to the command of the new Turkish 19th Division on the peninsula. It was an inspired choice.

On 19 February 1915 British Naval units began the campaign proper by seeking the progressive destruction of the forts guarding the south-western end of the straits. Such was the weakness of Turkish land defences at this time that a determined assault would have stood a solid chance of success in pressing forward to the high ground of Achi Baba. By 25 February this first phase was successful and the forts were abandoned by Turkish troops. Naval landing parties were able to complete the destruction of the guns within each fort. Success looked imminent[4]. Unfortunately it had only been decided, on 16 February, that an expeditionary land force would be formed. Initially it was planned to comprise that force of 50,000 men. None were available in February.

In this uneasy situation the Turkish navy held an ace within the deadly game being played in the Aegean approaches. On the night of 7 March the Turkish mine-layer *Nousret* managed to lay, undetected by the Allied forces, twenty mines parallel to the Asiatic coast on the south of the Dardanelles. Unaware of this development the Allied preparations continued until the dramatic events of 18 March. Just before this second phase of the campaign was opened the health of the commander of the British Eastern Mediterranean Squadron, Admiral Carden, broke down, necessitating his immediate replacement by Admiral de Robeck.

18 March was the date set for the naval forcing of the Narrows at Chanak Kale. Eighteen battleships, fourteen of them British and four French, entered the straits and opened fire at 11.30 am at a range of 14,000 yards (8 miles or 13 kilometres). The battleships quickly closed to what, in naval terms, was point

---

4. At this stage, early February 1915, preparations for a military landing were being made. Australians and New Zealanders were training in Egypt. The Naval Division was also available and a Regular Division from the UK. Greece contributed Lemnos island as a base.

blank range only a mile from the shore. As was revealed on many subsequent occasions during the campaign this exchange of fire between naval vessels and land based artillery revealed a significant difficulty for the British forces. All battleships had been constructed to fire at other battleships across a flat expanse of sea. In firing at targets on land it was clear that the high velocity and low trajectory of the shells made it nigh on impossible to hit mobile artillery hidden within and protected by hills and gullies. Nevertheless, in little more than two hours the inner forts seemed to have been overwhelmed by the heaviest fire from the *Inflexible*, *Queen Mary* and French ships including the *Bouvet*. It was time for the older vessels, pre Dreadnought designs, to move in behind the minesweepers to force the Narrows.

This moment, 1.45 pm on 18 March, 1915, was indeed a turning point in the war against Turkey. Were the Narrows to have been forced and had Allied naval vessels sailed into the Sea of Marmara then the Turkish capital city of Constantinople would have been under direct bombardment. The effect of such a circumstance will always be incalculable speculation. However, it would certainly have altered the way in which the subsequent Gallipoli landings were undertaken – even if they had been thought necessary at all.

As the *Bouvet* began to withdraw, in order to allow the second rank of battleships forward, she ran into the Nousret's mines. Within seconds the great ship blew up with the loss of 680 lives, only 21 of her crew being saved. Nevertheless, the minesweepers pushed on. This was the time when the balance still lay with the Allied fleet. Although fire from howitzer batteries and the remaining guns within the inner forts still made progress slow, progress there nevertheless was. However, further setbacks were close at hand to crush British naval willpower. At 4.11 pm the battlecruiser *Inflexible* struck a mine near Chanak Kale and took no further part as she limped away. Three minutes after *Inflexible* was struck the old battleship *Irresistible* was also put out of action. Most of her crew were transferred to the great battleship *Queen Elizabeth*.

Admiral de Robeck took the decision to break off the action.

In the aftermath *Inflexible* steamed slowly away to Tenedos. Another older battleship, *Ocean*, ordered to try and tow the *Irresistible* to safety, was herself struck by a mine. Both ships sank in the ensuing night although their crews were saved. Thus three major capital ships, HMS *Ocean*, HMS *Irresistible* and the French *Bouvet* were sunk whilst, HMS *Inflexible* and the *Suffren* and *Gaulois* were severely damaged. One third of the fleet had been lost. Allied naval resolve was dealt a severe blow by this effective deployment of simple

Kilid Bahr fort on the north bank of The Narrows, opposite Chanak Kale. (opposite)
This is the very essence of the 1915 Gallipoli campaign. Today Chanak Kale is the most important administrative centre in this area. That is no accident. The locale is a vital frontier on the face which mainland Turkey presents to Europe and the Mediterranean Sea. The Gallipoli peninsula is an integral part of the Canakkale Province of Turkey and what distinguishes this place is the narrowness of these waters.

Opposite Chanak Kale on the peninsula lies Kilid Bahr. Since the mid-16th century there had been forts whose purpose was to dominate the straits here. Even low-velocity medieval cannons were able to throw cannonballs from one shore to the other, creating an effective barrier to shipping.

By the autumn of 1914 the Young Turks were getting themselves into a war which was far too big for them, formally declaring war on the Triple Entente on 12 November 1914 but effectively in on the side of the Central Powers since 29 October. Once European war became a reality this location became immeasurably more important. Here, and at Constantinople or modern Istanbul, Turkish control of the water determined Russia's military and economic access to the Mediterranean Sea. In late 1914 that control was derived from howitzers, sea mines, torpedo tubes, anti-submarine nets and searchlights. At that time Russia's Black Sea fleet was of little significance and the arrival of the Goeben *and* Breslau, *on 11 August, gave Turkey a marked naval superiority which immediately proved to be of great significance in the Sea of Marmara and the Black Sea.*

Thus, if the British Fleet could force The Narrows, and subsequently the Bosphorus at Constantinople, then those German vessels could be sunk, armaments could be sent directly to Russia's hard-pressed forces via the Black Sea, the third of a million tons of shipping which were bottled up in those waters could be released and, in return, Russia's grain would become available to feed the Allied troops along the Western Front. It was further expected that such a defeat would create discord and revolutionary fervour in Constantinople, ending Turkish involvement in the war and bringing the Christian Balkan countries into the war on the Allied side. It was an enticing prospect.

technology. It was a humiliating defeat for Allied and especially British naval strategy. The withdrawal of a significant arm of the world's most powerful fleet was a turning point in the campaign to force the Narrows.

The perverse thing is that so few casualties had been suffered. In the context of what was to come, both at Gallipoli and in France and Flanders, the losses experienced on 18 March had been negligible, just 61 killed and wounded on board the British fleet, 600 in the French, almost all on board the *Bouvet*. Inexplicably these losses, trivial in the appalling catalogue of Great

War casualties, ensured that there would be no British follow-up action. The failure of Admiral de Robeck to sustain the attack into 19 March was the first major error in the campaign, since the Turks were by then close to defeat. Much of their ammunition was expended with no hope of replacement. Gun crews were exhausted and demoralised. Insufficient troops were available on or near the peninsula to mount an adequate defence. This should have been the moment when the British and French naval assault was pressed home with vigour and an amphibious landing mounted.

But in the unusual world of naval strategy, where the loss of capital ships was potentially disastrous, this was a naval defeat.

From now on the objective of forcing the Narrows and allowing access to the Sea of Marmara would have to be undertaken by land forces devoid of any element of surprise. Perversely, 18 March had been the date upon which the Gallipoli land forces commander arrived in the area. His first taste of the area was therefore one of bitter defeat. He was Sir Ian Hamilton, a Scot and career soldier whom many, including the Germans, regarded as an exceptionally talented man, one of the most brilliant commanders of the day. He was a former aide to Kitchener but was only given a rudimentary brief by 'K' about the ultimate aims of the campaign. Nevertheless, doubts soon began to emerge as to whether Hamilton's personality was sufficiently resolute for the rigours of such a complex and arduous mandate. He would have to command two very strong-willed subordinate generals who were contrasting and dominating figures in their own right. Lieutenant General William Birdwood was in command of the Australian and New Zealand Army Corps, the ANZACs. Birdwood was widely respected by his officers and men, for whom he had both regard and sensitivity. Sir Aylmer Hunter Weston commanded the British 29th Division. He was a hard and clinical man whose reputation for compounding errors grew throughout this campaign.

The landing strategy was endorsed by a meeting between Hamilton and de Robeck aboard the *Queen Elizabeth* on 22 March. The ground campaign would therefore become a means to an end – that is to the clearance of mines from The Narrows, the overcoming of associated Turkish infantry and artillery units and the consequential unopposed entry of the Eastern Mediterranean Squadron to the shores of Constantinople at the Bosphorus.

Even to the untutored eye, any campaign on the Gallipoli peninsula would face difficulties. It was some distance from the island base of Lemnos; the supply of such a major concentration of troops was therefore fraught with risk. The evacuation of casualties would be difficult. Water was effectively non-existent to invading troops. Heat, alien insect and animal life forms and the presence of hot climate diseases meant that the men would have to be given respite from its inhospitable environment. And almost as an aside there were many thousands of determined Turkish soldiers, fighting on their own familiar territory, whose supply and lines of communication were, by contrast, relatively assured.

For nearly six weeks after 18 March there was little or no offensive naval action against the Turkish defences which were being refined and developed on the Gallipoli peninsula. Such inertia was destined to have catastrophic consequences for the troops whose task it would ultimately be to storm the beaches and fight their way across that inhospitable terrain. Liman von Sanders now had some 80,000 Turkish troops under his command, although only a small proportion of that figure were established at the western end of the Gallipoli peninsula. Their combat effectiveness was hugely underestimated by Hamilton. During this period the Allied land forces were concentrated onto the island of Lemnos. Amongst them the 29th Division were a hardened regular army unit. Like the ANZACs they were genuinely tough and grimly resolved to do their duty. Their island base lay some fifty miles west of Gallipoli. In its fine natural harbour, Mudros, hundreds of vessels of every kind were assembled. This was to be the most ambitious amphibious landing in history but insufficient time had been devoted to the necessary preparation and loading of the equipment.

In any case what this agglomeration of vessels lacked was the right equipment. There was no comparable event in Britain's recent military past from which to draw lessons. And in all honesty the 'right equipment' simply did not exist. No armoured landing craft were available. The initial artillery support would be fired by naval guns whose shells' shallow trajectories were of little use against well-sited trenches[5]. Those supply vessels which existed had been loaded without reference to what would be needed in the first few hours of the assault. There were minimal numbers of artillery pieces available to the troops who would land.

On the night of 24 April the flotilla of transports, lighters, battleships and minesweepers left Mudros harbour, and the nearby Tenedos island, at 10.00 pm. Their destiny was less than ten hours away. To the north were ships carrying the Royal Naval Division bound for the Gulf of Saros where they would make a demonstration, designed to divide the Turkish defences, at Bulair. Further south was a French squadron heading for the Asiatic shores at Kum Kale, south of the Gallipoli peninsula. The French would land close to the historic site of Troy. The positions facing the anticipated main landings on the tip of the Gallipoli peninsula, at X, W and V beaches, were reached in total darkness at 3.30 am.

Half an hour later the troops were filing down the gangways into the waiting tows. There was no sound. The peninsula was shrouded in mist. The calm was almost penitent in its expectancy.

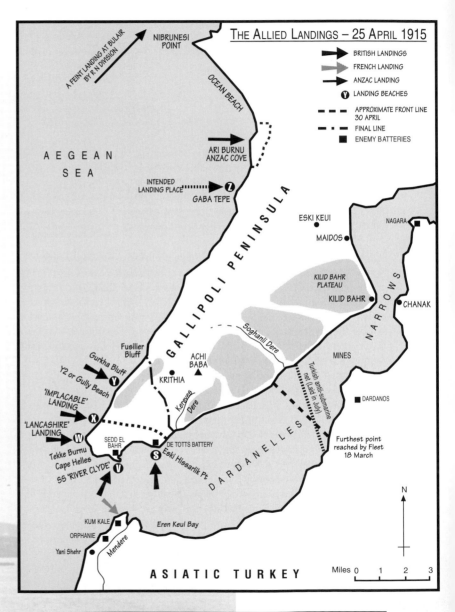

5. By contrast the Turkish land-based artillery made use of howitzers whose steeply plunging shell trajectories were well suited to the task in hand.

CHAPTER TWO

GALLIPOLI 2

Our Own Wooden Horse

On 22 April 1915 the Second Battle of Ypres began. That grim episode in western Belgium was quite capable of stretching the British Army's resources in Flanders almost to breaking point. Yet the imminent landings at Gallipoli were about to distort the delicate balance even further. It was, throughout the Gallipoli campaign, an ongoing problem that the War Cabinet found themselves unable to commit sufficient military assets. This cautious, almost half-hearted, approach would ultimately lead to disaster. The ill-fated Gallipoli land campaign was thus to be launched during a period of acute munitions shortage on the Western Front. The British artillery in Flanders had barely 20% of their daily shell requirements. By contrast the French held each mile of their sectors of the Western Front with roughly twice the numbers of artillery pieces as the British, and had sufficient shells to make those pieces effective. The divisions which were about to land at Gallipoli were equipped with just 118 of the 306 guns which were their correct establishment. The men had insufficient artillery pieces and insufficient ammunition for those guns. It was a shortage which persisted throughout the campaign.

What should have been said, very firmly at that moment in time, is that nobody liked the Western Front, its mortars and gas, its trenches, its 'fuckin' artillery', its casualties and its fantastic reluctance to move. Yet by trying to bypass that terrible killing ground the progenitors of the Gallipoli campaign were ignoring some vital and inevitable conclusions about the changed nature of war. The effective use of quick-firing artillery, the development of trench systems, the mass production of reliable machine guns and the widespread deployment of barbed wire defences made traditional infantry assaults with fixed bayonets untenable. An outline of those tactical conditions

Throughout the Gallipoli campaign the role of the navy in providing support was crucial. Unfortunately the trajectory of their large calibre shells meant that bombardments proved ineffective against carefully sited Turkish infantry trenches and mobile artillery pieces.

was already in place on Gallipoli where the Turkish army, prepared and tutored by Liman von Sanders, proved itself no less capable of deploying such measures than any European counterpart. Further defences would develop with accelerated speed within hours of the landings.

Consolidation would therefore be the name of the British game[1].

To get things off to an inauspicious start the landings at Helles were destined to take place in daylight. Naval fears about local currents and reefs made them hesitant about landing a large body of troops under the cloak of darkness. We will never know what might have happened if such an endeavour had been undertaken successfully before the flush of dawn gave sight and advantage to the Gallipoli defences. Speculation suggests that well drilled and hardened regular troops, such as those which abounded within the 29th Division, would have held their discipline and shape better than the recently retrained units which opposed them that morning.

The main assault was to be delivered against the westernmost tip of the peninsula, around the Cape Helles, by the 29th Division. Attached were two battalions of the Royal Naval Division. The landing would be effected on five beaches. Running anti-clockwise around the tip from north to south they were: Y, X, W, V and S. The ANZACs were to be thrown in further to the north on the European coast of the peninsula at Ari Burnu. The whole enterprise would be supported and covered by the firepower of a considerable armada of naval vessels; 18 battleships, 12 cruisers and 29 destroyers, of which five were French vessels. French ground forces would also be involved in a landing at Kum Kale on the Turkish mainland opposite the tip of the peninsula[2]. The tactics were right: multiple landings, with a feint attack at Bulair to confuse. But the execution of those tactics was, in the event, lamentably poor.

Anzac Cove. *(above and opposite)*
What an improbable and remarkable place. The beaches and their spectacularly elevated surroundings create a fitting testimony to the determination and sheer tenacity of the citizen soldiers who fought their way ashore here on the morning of April 25 1915. High above the waterline these gullies and rocky slopes became a tenuous, blighted home to thousands of astonishingly resilient Australians and New Zealanders. Eighty-five years on there are fewer than a handful of men alive who knew of this place's unforgiving circumstances and who understood the devoted camaraderie and anguish which were inextricably linked to the ANZAC campaign here. The utter finality of the nearby cemeteries underscores the quite palpable pain felt by friends who had to leave without the campaign being resolved in their favour. There are so many young men's graves here, both marked and unknown, so very far from their home. I often wonder whether it would be possible to so galvanise and motivate a nation that it would be prepared, today, to fight a similar campaign, to accept its losses and swallow the bitter pill of defeat. Many come here from all walks of life to ponder those questions. It is an unrivalled place in which to so do.

---

1. Consolidation meant the process of digging new trenches, and/or repairing shell shattered trenches, in newly captured positions, placing new wire entanglements in front, establishing lines of communication and supply to the rear, sending forward patrols and outposts to identify the nearest enemy positions.

2. These French forces came under Hamilton's command. The French were a cosmopolitan team which fought well throughout. Having landed successfully at Kum Kale they were soon ordered to withdraw from the Asiatic coast in order to reinforce the British at Helles in time for the First Battle of Krithia.

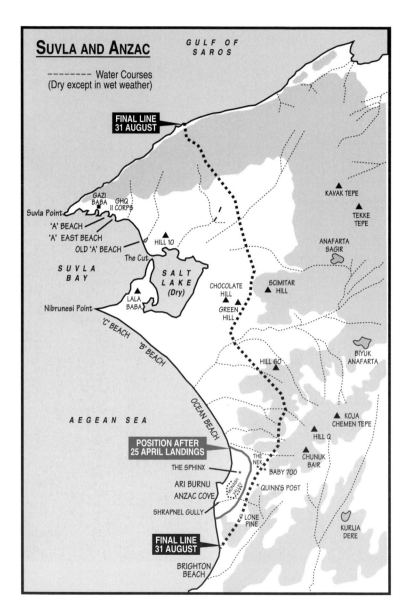

SUVLA AND ANZAC

GULF OF SAROS

------- Water Courses
(Dry except in wet weather)

FINAL LINE 31 AUGUST

KAVAK TEPE

GAZI BABA
GHQ II CORPS

Suvla Point

TEKKE TEPE

'A' BEACH
'A' EAST BEACH
OLD 'A' BEACH

The Cut

HILL 10

ANAFARTA SAGIR

SUVLA BAY

SALT LAKE (Dry)

CHOCOLATE HILL

SCIMITAR HILL

Nibrunesi Point

LALA BABA

GREEN HILL

'C' BEACH

'B' BEACH

BIYUK ANAFARTA

HILL 60

OCEAN BEACH

AEGEAN SEA

KOJA CHEMEN TEPE

HILL Q

POSITION AFTER 25 APRIL LANDINGS

THE NEK
BABY 700

CHUNUK BAIR

THE SPHINX

ARI BURNU
ANZAC COVE

QUINN'S POST

SHRAPNEL GULLY

MONASH VALLEY

LONE PINE

KURIJA DERE

FINAL LINE 31 AUGUST

BRIGHTON BEACH

The ANZAC Landings.

The ANZAC landings were planned to take place well before the full light of dawn. The site chosen for their beachhead lay between two promontories, Gaba Tepe to the south and Ari Burnu. North of Ari Burnu the beach backs onto an area of impossibly precipitous cliffs and aretes leading steeply eastwards to the hills of Baby 700, Battleship Hill, Chunuk Bair and Koja Chemen Tepe - the Sari Bair Ridge.

The strain on the men had been immense. Each was heavily laden, a rifle, pack, 200 rounds of ammunition and three days' rations. A total weight of 88 lbs. (40 kilos). Even the Official History, which usually makes little if any reference to the sentiments felt by the ordinary soldier, speaks freely about the tensions. They must be equally applicable to those felt at the Helles landings which were soon to be made at dawn on the peninsula's tip.

The Sphinx from Plugge's Plateau. (opposite)
Just a few yards east of Anzac Cove the ground rears up in a spectacular outburst of promontories and declivities. The most dramatic of all is the Sphinx, a steeply eroded and suddenly terminated arete facing the North Beach. This is the site of the First Anzac ridge. These were the cliffs and torrid slopes which made this location such an unlikely landing place. The explanation of that inappropriate landing to the north of Anzac Cove has exercised historians for many years. Suffice it to say, as a direct consequence of that error, the topography of the ground facing the ANZACs on landing was even more severe than need have been the case.

With time, care and a guide you can find your way inland across the depths of Monash Gully and up onto the rugged outcrops of the Second Anzac ridge - Quinn's Post, Courtney's Post and the Bloody Angle. The two ridges came together at a critical juncture - The Nek. Crossing that crucial point, just two miles north-east of Anzac Cove, takes you on towards the summit of Chunuk Bair from which you can look uninterruptedly across the Dardanelles and into Asia. This is Sari Bair, or yellow hill, a ridge much coveted by the British. Along the way to its highest ground lie Baby 700, Battleship Hill and the Rhododendron Spur. In winter any sudden heavy rains on these slopes produce a torrential current of water which gushes down the deres and gullies to spill into the sea. One of the gullies' legendary names, the apt Valley of Despair, reminds everyone who comes here what a grim journey it was from the shores of the Aegean to the deadly terror of the trenches which were established east of here. Along that little-trod high ground the few determined visitors who persist come across the lonely detritus of war, water bottles, rusted fragments of rifles and cartridge cases. Below, in the jagged confines of the valley floors which edge their way inland, it is not unusual, as at Verdun, to come across the bony remnants of a human life squandered here. These are inaccessible places. Shepherds and the dedicated workers of the Commonwealth War Graves Commission are now its natural inhabitants.

'The loading of the boats had begun at 1.30 am. Thenceforward for three hours, till half past four, the men sat motionless and silent, so tightly wedged together that they could scarcely move their limbs, heading towards the unknown. Whether the landing would be a surprise, or whether an army was waiting for them, was a question none could answer.'[3]

As at Helles the troops were towed towards their destination behind small steamboats. As they approached the coastline the vessels were beginning to bunch together. It was 4.00 am when the shore became faintly visible but here the outline presence of Ari Burnu on the lead vessels' port (left) bow confused

The Diggers as Australia's citizen army became known were ingenious and resilient soldiers. This photograph shows Australians and men of the Royal Naval Division using a periscope rifle at Anzac.

the sailors. Thinking themselves too far to the south, that is too close to Gaba Tepe, Lieutenant Waterlow began to steer to the north. Other vessels realised the error and crossed the wake of Waterlow's tows until they were to his starboard (right) thus inextricably mixing the units. At 4.45 the tows were cast off and sailors rowed each boat ashore. Three left tows carrying most of the 11th Battalion ground onto the shingle 200 metres north of Ari Burnu, under the near vertical slab slopes of the Sphinx, whilst the remaining boats got ashore around the headland[4] which formed the northernmost promontory defining a small bay, the legendary Anzac Cove.

'We were supposed to land on a shelving shore, with cultivated ground, and an orchard running almost on to the beach. Judge my horror, when in the half light I saw we were being towed direct for a narrow strip of beach, with almost inaccessible cliffs rising straight from the beach to a height of 200 feet. ... At last our boat grounded and I jumped out as I thought into two feet of water. It was up to my neck, and under I went. I got up, scrambled into about two feet of water and waved the boys on and they all jumped out quickly enough who could...We climbed up the beach and lay doggo for a few seconds while everyone took off his pack and got a breather.'

Everywhere that these men looked up they were faced by a phalanx of cliffs. The structure is akin to a great bowl, formed by Walker's Ridge, Russell's Top and Plugge's Plateau. Dominating the centre was an impossibly vertical feature known as the Sphinx because of its uncanny similarity to the Egyptian feature which these Australians had known well just a few short weeks before[5]. Within minutes the natural aggression and confidence of these remarkable men overwhelmed caution. They were instilled with the need to get forward - an instinct which they had been imbued with for weeks before the landing - and now began to scale the cliffs above their improbable beachhead.

'Then, round a winding, precipitous path, up, up, up, we charged. Not a rifle had been loaded (by strict order) and our boys did not waste their breath cheering until we got to the top. Then a wild coo-ee and the bayonet.'

[Source. Captain Dixon Hearder, quoted in *Gallipoli*, Steel.]

The troops which formed the second wave from the destroyers stuck to their allotted landing places, thereby further confusing the chain of command. Notwithstanding that immense difficulty, the mêlée of citizen soldiers threw themselves into the attack with boundless vigour.

3. *Military Operations. Gallipoli.* pp 172.

4. There is a fascinating insight into these events in *Gallipoli*, Nigel Steel, Battleground Europe Series. pp 105-113. Leo Cooper, Pen & Sword Books Ltd. 1999. The illustrative quotations are taken from that work.

5. Since their arrival in the Mediterranean the ANZACs had been training in the Egyptian sand dunes.

'There was not two men of the same battalion together. The men did all on their own initiative, which was greatly to their credit. They crawled, climbed, ran and struggled over boulders, hills, valleys and dales, ever going up and up this enormously high mountain like a cliff for it was a fearful height...Up and down we went, up, up, for ever it seemed; this time to the summit which at last we reached and then we dashed along after the Turks who we could see clearly now in the rising of the sunlight. Here a tremendous report came echoing all around. We, for the moment, wondered what had happened. The ground seemed steady. Then it dawned on us. It was the warships that had commenced to back us up. The good old *Triumph* had sent [a] 10 inch flyer to Jacko at Gaba Tepe fort and then another in quick succession. The Turks hastened a bit and we also took a faster run and, the result of this splendid 'music'? We let go a mighty British cheer and 'cooeed' to our cobbers below who 'cooeed' back. This Australian cry must have put the fear of Allah on to Jacko, for he doubled his efforts at running and so did we. '

[Source. Anonymous soldier of C Company, 11th Battalion AIF. Quoted in *Gallipoli*, Steel.]

That high ground, east of Anzac Cove, was Plugge's Plateau from where the Australians could see a detachment of some 30 - 40 Turks disappearing into a scrub-filled ravine on the far side. Some Australians charged into the ravine. Wiser heads waited whilst some semblance of order was restored to the mixture of units. In the burgeoning daylight the erroneous site of the landings was clearly visible. 400 Plateau, which should have faced the men, lay a thousand yards south east of Plugge's Plateau.

To the north-east of Plugge's Plateau a determined group of some 50 men formed from the 12th, and remnants of the 11th, Australian battalion under the command of Colonel Clarke fought their way up and onto Russell's Top across which they forced the Turks back towards The Nek and Baby 700. Clarke was killed, but by mid-morning his men had reached the rear slopes of Battleship Hill, but that was as far as they reached. It was here that Mustafa Kemal, charged with the defence of these hills, and in command of the Turkish 19th Division, restored the morale of his men and brought forward the 57th Regiment's three battalions. Gradually the ANZACs were pushed back across Baby 700 where fighting for its summit then swayed back and forth throughout the early afternoon. By late afternoon it was apparent that the Turks' overwhelming strength could not be resisted, the forward ANZAC units being so depleted that the few men left withdrew past The Nek onto Russell's Top where their lines in this area remained fixed throughout the Gallipoli campaign.

The first day's battle for the security of higher ground inland had thus been fought on the initiative of individual soldiers and their junior officers. The separation of units meant that in many cases platoons were commanded by NCOs around whom the steep slopes and dense thickets of scrub meant that it was impossible for such inexperienced men to maintain direction or control.

The Turkish troops now gathered in strength on their higher ground. The Australians' objectives, Hill 971 and Mal Tepe, withered into a distant haze. By the end of the day the position could be better evaluated:

- 15,000 men ashore.
- 2,000 casualties.

Dozens of decomposing Turkish bodies litter the rocky terrain of No Man's Land in front of the Anzac positions.

- A difficult beach secured which suffered greatly from hostile observation, both to the north and south, making the anchorages and supply of materiel hazardous.
- Australian and New Zealand Troops in positions which were deemed barely practicable for defence. The ANZACs' frontage was just one and a half miles in length (two kilometres). Its greatest depth between the front lines and the sea was no more than a thousand yards (950 meters). Nevertheless, at least 10,000 men were available to hold this position which would be a tightly confined home to the ANZAC forces for the next three months.
- GHQ's aspirations in tatters. Hamilton's plans had underestimated both the topographical severity of the area and the fighting tenacity of 'Jacko' - the Turk.

- Great shortages of small arms ammunition, water and supporting artillery.
- Considerable Turkish casualties and dislocation.

Seldom indeed has the mettle of inexperienced troops been subjected to a more severe test than was that of the citizen soldiers of Australia and New Zealand on their first day of active service. Hazardous as a landing on an unknown shore must always be, the task of the 3rd Australian Brigade was made still more arduous by the unfortunate chance which carried it to a landing place of unexpected and unexampled severity. The battle which then began cannot be judged by the standards of any ordinary attack, where the troops, carefully assembled beforehand, start from a definite line, at a definite zero hour. Arriving piecemeal in boats, landing under fire where best they could, wading ashore in the dark, finding themselves in many cases

'W' Beach. (left and (opposite)

We will soon meet one officer of the Lancashire Fusiliers, Captain Ainsleigh Douglas 'Addy' Talbot. His narrative of how men in those thirty nervous cramped row boats coped with the landings manages to be both laconic and informative. His numerous letters provide evocative insights into the life of regular soldiers under his command and often, with a light and sensitive touch, raise serious issues. Many months before the events on W beach the Lancashire Fusiliers' men's minds had been concentrated on other matters. Talbot wrote of their fleshly pleasures, whilst in billets after their return from Indian service, soon after the outbreak of war.

'......our men are having the time of their lives in the billets; the whole place swarms with very pretty hat factory girls, not bad looking either, I should think that in nine months time there should be the makings of a new army in Nuneaton alone.'

Soon after the Gallipoli landings Addy Talbot would write again from hospital whilst recovering from an ankle injury. He knew how severely depleted were the ranks of men, perhaps expectant fathers, under his command. For many girls in that billet town eight months had passed since the Lancashire Fusiliers had passed through. Talbot understood well that many families were being created in less than propitious circumstances.

'I must say I feel sorry for the girls in Nuneaton if they really cared; but it will show that part of the country what a soldier does have to go through.'

Now at the far end of this extraordinary century, as we come to terms with another European war, I often wonder whether the enthusiasts for such conflict have learned Talbot's prescient lesson. Do we really know of just what 'a soldier does have to go through'? How poignant that the hurried couplings of lovers in the trauma of war in 1914 should give rise to a 'new army in Nuneaton' in 1915. Those children would grow, just in time, to be in the prime of their twenty-four years of life before events already pencilled onto the calendar for 1939-45 would swallow them up.

The view on the right shows a broader view of these piers on 'W' Beach and the outline of distant Kum Kale across the entrance to the Dardanelles.

confronted by unclimbable cliffs, hunting for a practicable line of ascent, and then scrambling up a difficult hillside covered with prickly scrub, it would have been hard indeed for units to avoid disintegration. The means of communicating orders and getting back information, always liable to interruption, were completely dislocated; the chain of command - none too strong at that time - was snapped. Individual groups of high-mettled men flung themselves forward on their own initiative; platoons and companies became fatally intermixed and the plans for each battalion's special task fell hopelessly to bits.

> 'Taking all these factors into consideration it may well be doubted whether even a division of veteran troops could have carried out a co-ordinated attack at ANZAC on the 25th April. The predominant feeling, which that astounding battlefield must always arouse in the military student who visits it, will be a sense of unstinted admiration for those untried battalions who did so exceedingly well. The magnificent physique, the reckless daring, and the fine enthusiasm of the Dominion troops on their first day of trial went far to counteract anything they lacked in training and war experience. The story of their landing will remain for all time amongst the proudest traditions of the Australian and New Zealand Forces.'[6]

Fine words, but in truth it would have been almost impossible to design a less promising beachhead. The terrain to the east was an ideal defensive position, littered with numerous ridges and deep ravines. Turkish forces were able to exploit this situation to great effect. The ANZACs faced the uncompromisingly dominant high ground of the Sari Bair Ridge and were supplied by sea approaches all too easily observed from the Turkish-held promontories at Lala Baba and Gaba Tepe. The ANZACs were in a desperately constrained and precarious position.

The 29th Division Landings.

The landings on Y beach were expected to threaten the Turkish lines of retreat if those units were to be forced eastwards by the British landings at X and W. The tragedy of this event is simple. It was inactivity, on the part of the 2,000 troops who got ashore without opposition, which saw the advantage slip away. For the first eleven hours they were unopposed. As the Official History laments '...throughout that period, they alone were equal in numbers to all the Turkish forces south of Achi Baba. Yet throughout the 25th the initial success remained unexploited.'[7] This was incredible. The men had landed

without a shot being fired at them from the shore. As Sir Ian Hamilton passed the beachhead later that day, en route from the ANZAC landings to Helles on board the battleship *Queen Elizabeth*, crowds of troops could be seen sitting astride the cliff edges. The morning was so quiet that the commanding officer of the Plymouth Battalion, Colonel Matthews, walked across the Gully Ravine south of Y beach to within 500 yards of Krithia village. It was seen to be unoccupied. The troops at Y beach remained fastened to the spot by their officers' inability to demonstrate offensive spirit. The only conceivable explanation is that he was out of contact with his superior officers, and that they were preoccupied with the far more difficult situations at the other beaches. Whatever, the inactivity at Y beach was lamentable and had serious consequences as events unfolded elsewhere.

The following morning, from 2.00 am onwards, Y beach was under severe Turkish counter-attack. Problems worsened after some naval shells fell short amongst the British troops, some of whom began to drift back towards the beach. Between 8 and 9.00 am the position worsened. To his great disappointment Hamilton, on board the *Queen Elizabeth*, could get no information from the ragged clusters of men on Y beach who were in the process of evacuation. Within hours, by mid-afternoon on 26 April, the British troops on Y beach were gone. The Official History uses language which is unusually emotive in describing the outcome of this ill-conducted event.

> 'In deciding to throw a force ashore at that point Sir Ian Hamilton would seem to have hit on the key of the whole situation...a bold advance from Y on the morning of the 25th April must have freed the southern beaches that morning, and ensured a decisive victory for the 29th Division...the results of the enterprise were heart-breaking.'[8]

The landings at three of the other four beaches were destined to be very different. The men were to be put ashore soon after daybreak in small craft towed behind powered vessels. Each landing would be supervised by a supporting mother ship (HMS *Implacable* at X beach, *Euralyus* at W, Fleet Sweeper No 1 at V and HMS *Cornwallis* at S beach on the southern coast at Morto Bay). The fleet opened a heavy bombardment of the southern end of the peninsula at 5.00 am and the landings began half an hour later. At V beach after the initial landings the collier *River Clyde*, carrying more than 2,000 men, was to be run aground allowing its complement of soldiers to charge out of specially constructed sally ports cut in the vessel's side.

The first task of the men landing at X, W and V was to capture the high

---

6. *Military Operations. Gallipoli.* pp 199-200

7. *Military Operations. Gallipoli.* Vol 1. pp 202. The Turkish strength in the area south west of Achi Baba during the first 24 hours of the landings was minimal - two battalions and a company of engineers!

8. *Military Operations. Gallipoli.* Vol 1. pp 215.

ground immediately to the east of the beaches, Hill 114, Hill 138 and Hill 141. The day's final objective was a line running across the peninsula including the dominant high ground of Achi Baba. Hunter Weston, commanding the 29th Division, wanted to capture all the high ground running due east of Achi Baba in order to have observation and some degree of artillery control to support any subsequent naval attack towards the Narrows. If all went well the village of Krithia would have been captured and the Turkish forces in the remainder of the peninsula would be in danger of being cut off from their retreat by the advance of the ANZACs from their landing at Gaba Tepe.

Throughout the first day the 29th Division's troops believed they were facing strong forces. They were wrong. Y beach was undefended. W and V were protected by just one company on each beach at S beach only one platoon, while at X beach - a post of just twelve men. However, the skill of the defenders had been in siting their positions to give maximum advantage to their machine guns. The defences at W were particularly well positioned. The Turkish troops' resolve was never in question.

The Royal Fusiliers' landing at X beach. This beach was on the northern side of the peninsula's tip. It was the smallest of the three landing sites at that tip. The sandy strip lay beneath a low crumbling cliff guarded by a detachment of just a dozen men. The supervising mother ship, HMS *Implacable*, maintained such an intensity of fire that the Royal Fusiliers' troops came ashore here without opposition. By 7.30 am the beach was secure and by 11.00 am the *Implacable's* sailors could see the troops on the summit of Hill 114. From their positions the Royal Fusiliers' officers could see across the peninsula's tip all the way to Morto Bay. Unfortunately insufficient men were landed at X beach to take advantage of that view and opportunity. Neither,

'...The angular outline of the beached River Clyde *became one of the lasting images of the Gallipoli campaign.'*

again unfortunately, were sufficient men available to press north-eastwards to join up with the groups now wasting precious time above Y beach.

The Lancashire Fusiliers' landing at W beach is an unrivalled example of soldierly and regimental gallantry. Fired at from three sides and facing complex entanglements of barbed wire and mines, the soldiers' determination to succeed carried them forward.

The 1st Battalion of the Lancashire Fusiliers were the first to land here although their numbers were cruelly thinned by accurate machine-gun and rifle fire which devastated the cutters carrying those men to shore. Captain A.D.Talbot's measured description of these events is a masterly understatement:

> 'I can tell you the sight of the peninsula being shelled by the fleet was grand with the sun rising above it all. We kicked off right outside the supporting ships and went in fairly fast until we were right under the cannon's mouth. The noise of the 10' etc were deafening. We never got a shot fired at us till the oars were tossed and then they started in earnest. The first bullet that struck the water brought up loud jeers from our men, but poor devils they little thought what they were in for....Tom Mannsell and Tommy were shot getting out of the boat. Clark was shot through the head sitting in the boat. I tell you I looked pretty slippy about getting ashore. I jumped overboard into five feet of water. I don't think the men realised how hot the fire was they were laughing and joking till the last.'[9]

Facing severe casualties inside the tightly packed boats, Talbot's men were ordered over the side well before reaching landfall. Although the waters were shallow, many were drowned under the weight of their packs and extra ammunition. Those who reached the beach often found their rifles useless, clogged with sand. It is one of the enduring images that soldiers had the presence of mind, while lying exposed on the beach under intense fire, to clean their rifles before getting on with the job again[10]. Such behaviour required immense personal discipline and courage.

In spite of the enormous difficulties, by 7.15 am a line had been established which made the beach secure from all but a few stray shots. Unfortunately this was the time when the brigadier commanding (Brigadier General Hare) was severely wounded. His successor, Lieutenant Colonel Newenham, was also badly wounded before he could take command. The men's fighting advance was therefore under the control of relatively junior officers, whose bravery and leadership were unmistakable but who lacked the overall perspective to give direction to the advance. Perhaps even more crucially the Fusiliers' numbers were now so depleted that it proved impossible to link up with the V beach landings.

Throughout this campaign the beach, initially so unimaginatively labelled 'W', became known hereafter as 'Lancashire Landing' following an initiative of rare imagination by Hamilton. Six Victoria Crosses had been won 'before breakfast' by the officers and men of the 1st Battalion of the Lancashire Fusiliers[11] which had lost 11 officers and 350 men in getting ashore.

The *River Clyde* and the V beach landings. This beach was the most significant of the landing sites, it being expected that more than 2,800 troops would be deployed here. Afterwards the angular outline of the beached *River Clyde* became one of the lasting images of the Gallipoli campaign. The beach and rocky spit where the collier was to be run aground were dominated on the east by the old fort and the village of Sedd-el-Bahr and on the west by Fort No.1. The ground above the beach forms a natural amphitheatre. The defences, which had been placed here to harass any attempted landing, included three barbed wire complexes, two pom-pom guns and four machine guns, as well as cleverly sited trenches and ruins from which riflemen were able to operate undetected.

Mistakenly it had been presumed that the advance barrage fired from HMS *Albion* would devastate the willingness of the Turkish troops here to resist. The terrible reality was that as the first tows carrying the Dublin Fusiliers, which preceded the *River Clyde*, approached the shore the boats were riven by an overwhelming hail of machine-gun and rifle fire. Within seconds some of the boats were drifting aimlessly, their occupants dead. Wounded survivors drowned as they stumbled in the water. The few who survived were almost all hit as they waded ashore to take shelter beneath a grassy embankment at the head of the sand.

The subsequent beaching of the *River Clyde* was an example of too complex a plan failing under the pressure of events. Trapped within its steel the Munsters had no escape from the hail of machine-gun fire which would inevitably be fired at any attempts by the heavily laden men to clamber out of the vessel. Only enduring heroism from Commander Unwin, Able Seaman William Williams and Midshipman George Drewry enabled a temporary walkway made from two of the lighters to be placed, enabling some of the

---

9. These words were penned in letter to Addy Talbot's friend, Captain Tom Slingsby. They are held in the Department of Documents at the Imperial War Museum.

10. All soldiers carried a small oil bottle and cotton wadding or 'pull through' which could be drawn along the barrel of their rifle to clear away any grit or sand from within.

11. Captain C.Bromley. Captain R.R.Willis. Sergeant A.Richards. Lance-Sergeant F.E.Stubbs. Corporal J.E.Grimshaw. Private W.Keneally.

'V' beach (opposite)
The wreckage of piers in the foreground with the entrance to the Dardanelles in the background.

men to launch forth. Within minutes the casualties amounted to 70% of those who had attempted to land. By 9.00 am it was clear that the landings on V beach were stalled. Inside the *River Clyde* 1,000 men remained trapped. They were indeed fortunate. Had the Turkish defenders possessed any field artillery capable of being brought to bear on the unarmoured ship's hull then the troops inside would have been annihilated. Outside, as the water lapped against the spits of rock and the gunwales of the tows, the few observers could see the colour of the water running deep red for some 50 yards out to sea. As the last sun drained away from that first day's terrible carnage it became possible for the *River Clyde's* soldiers to come ashore unmolested under the cover of darkness.

The landings of the South Wales Borderers at S beach. As at Y beach, on the northern shore, the landings at S beach, facing the Asiatic coast, were another opportunity lost. Here three companies of the South Wales Borderers had been landed with minimal opposition under cover of fire from HMS *Cornwallis'* guns. By 8.00 am the whole position was captured along with almost all the small Turkish garrison. The South Wales Borderers thus outnumbered the one company of Turkish soldiers defending the Sedd-el-Bahr positions above V beach, 2,500 yards to the west, and should have been able to disrupt that defence. Unfortunately the officer in charge was duped by a Turkish prisoner's claim that they had 2,000 men in reserve. Colonel Casson decided to dig in. During the next two days his party was unmolested – his casualties amounting to 15 killed and fewer than fifty wounded.

Of course, with the benefit of hindsight, it is all too easy to be critical of commanders whose judgement was overwhelmed by the mélange of critical moments, the anguish of bad news and the stress of the unexpected. In reality the failure to capitalise on the successes at S and Y beaches had much to do with the inability of relatively primitive forms of communication to cope with the speed of events. If it had been possible to land substantially more troops at these two points on S and Y beaches, under orders to press resolutely towards Achi Baba, then the outcome of 25 April's events could have been very different. As it was the day turned from bad to worse. Critical casualties amongst key officers, poor intelligence about the strength of Turkish opposition, a belief that action elsewhere would resolve localised and seemingly insurmountable problems all led to a lack of impetus. Hamilton's first test had thus ended in failure - failure which came to typify the rest of the campaign.

The neglect of that opportunity to seize the initiative on the first day would come back to haunt the invaders time after time, every day and night of the subsequent campaign.

◆ ◆ ◆

For the wounded their trials were only just beginning. It quickly became apparent that inadequate arrangements had been made for the evacuation and treatment of casualties. The nearest Allied hospital facilities were in Egypt or further back at Malta. Either destination required a lengthy and uncomfortable journey. There were, quite simply, insufficient hospital ships with medical, surgical and nursing facilities on board to get the casualties to these destinations. On the night of 25 April, the day of the first landings, it proved impossible to get casualties away. Men lay on the beaches, badly wounded and clad only in battle-filthied light desert kit. On the evening of the 26th the first batch of wounded were taken from ANZAC beach. It was

Achi Baba. (opposite)
From X beach, on the northern side of the peninsula's tip, it is five miles or eight kilometres to Achi Baba. The hill is flanked by broad-shouldered high ground on both its north-western and south-eastern sides, making it a formidable obstacle and a dominant observation platform. The hill does not figure as a significant height on most relief maps, being only 709 feet at its highest point. These smoothly rounded uplands are in stark contrast to the vertiginous cliffs which faced the ANZACs from the onset at their landings. The plans which were drawn up to define the objectives of the initial landings at Helles made plain that Achi Baba was to be captured by the close of the first day's fighting.

Between X beach and Achi Baba lie the two key features of the terrain on this western tip of the Gallipoli peninsula. Running from north-east to south-west are four parallel gullies or deres. These clefts carry winter water away from the Achi Baba ridge but are arid in summer. Above and between the deres are spurs of slightly elevated ground running down from the higher ground of the ridge. These spurs are almost imperceptible beneath the scrub but their control gave a vital advantage to the Turkish defence. The ground provides little by way of nutrients. In the drought of summer, if the land is left unirrigated by local farmers, a steady spindrift of dust and sand are left to blow ceaselessly on the hot breeze. Dessicated brushwood and coarse grasses eke out an existence here, supplemented by spectacular outbursts of colour when spring rains first draw forth the germination of a multitude of colourful plants.

British and French troops were condemned to months of misery in this low-lying hell by virtue of the British High Command's failure to utilise the benefits of surprise. Once the forts at Sedd-el-Bahr and Kum Kale were prematurely devastated in the enormous bombardment of 19 February it was clear to all that an attempt on The Narrows was planned, yet little attempt had been made to expedite the creation of a landing force. When that force was finally assembled, in time to be put ashore on 25 April, the Turkish defences across this vulnerable part of the peninsula had been made ready. Achi Baba was never captured by the British.

not until three days later that the four shiploads of wounded reached Alexandria. Within a week the Australian hospitals in Cairo were flooded with wounded men.

During the first days of the campaign there were periods during which there were no hospital ships off ANZAC[12]. Hired transport vessels were pressed into action. These were 'the black ships' which were often still carrying horses which it had not been possible to offload on the beachheads. The wounded were necessarily laid in areas where the horse litter was saturated with equine urine. There were no bedpans, paper or anaesthetics. The stench of fouled clothing, of gangrenous infection and ammonia-laden air pervaded the decks throughout. One of the worst vessels, the *Lutzow*, took on 500 wounded. Its captain was German and the crew 'Levantines, Greeks, Italians and Turks.' They gave little help to the wounded. In truth even if they had been better disposed to the plight of these desperate men, the crews had

12. The principal vessel, *Gascon*, was in transit to and from Alexandria.

little expertise. At best there were a tiny band of nursing staff and doctors on board to help.

✦ ✦ ✦

During the succeeding week the British efforts at the tip of the Gallipoli peninsula enabled them to form a continuous line and set about attempting to capture the village of Krithia. By 6 May another attempt, the Second Battle of Krithia, was made amidst mounting British casualties. At ANZAC the fighting was intense from the first day of the landings. The following morning, 26 April, the Turks attacked in strength across Russell's Top and Pope's Hill. In the confined space available the ANZAC HQ was established on the lower slopes of Plugge's Plateau. A roll call on 30 April revealed that

The limited numbers of Artillery pieces, especially howitzers, was a constant problem for the British Army at Gallipoli. These gunners are firing from positions at Helles.

Little has changed amongst the simple and dignified farms which punctuate the landscape below Achi Baba near the village of Krithia.

179 officers and 4,752 troops had become casualties. The following day, 1 May, a massive Turkish counter-attack was launched, again under the direction of Mustafa Kemal. That failed to dislodge the Turks' persistent opponents and allowed an ANZAC attempt, the following day, to attack Baby 700 and to occupy some of the eastern parts of 400 Plateau. Soon Liman von Sanders realised that closing the gaps between the trenches across 400 Plateau would prevent the relatively inaccurate naval guns from being deployed against Turkish trenches. It was a clever tactic and one which produced conditions of unusual proximity between the front line positions here on Gallipoli.

Sanders' greatest fear was that the ANZACs would break out of their precarious home and cross the peninsula, thereby cutting off the Turkish troops facing the Helles positions. On 19 May at 3.00 am the Turks launched the newly rested 2nd Division against the ANZAC positions. By 5.00 am Turkish casualties had mounted to 10,000, but the casualties were wasted. The ANZAC forces were neither split nor driven back towards the water. Within hours the heat produced a wretched stench which hung over the already flyblown corpses. So serious a threat to health was the overwhelming number of corpses in No Man's Land here at ANZAC that it could not be overlooked. An armistice was arranged to bury the dead from both sides of the conflict. By the end of May allied casualties at Gallipoli stood at 38,000[13].

Early June saw the third and final, predictably unsuccessful, attempt to capture Krithia. By late June the conflict reached a pinnacle of ferocity with massive Turkish losses as they strove to push the Allied forces from the peninsula during counter-attacks on 30 June and 2 July. The campaign was now in a state of equilibrium with both sides seemingly unable to defeat each other, whilst the Allies were stuck with the unpalatable notion of having to withdraw.

This stalemate led to plans to break out of ANZAC with attacks on the higher ground of Chunuk Bair. Diversions could be employed at Suvla, Lone Pine and The Nek. However, mounting losses at ANZAC meant that Suvla Bay would became a far more significant proposal. It would be left to General Birdwood to break that deadlock .

The desperate fighting at the end of June in the Helles sector again produced a need to evacuate large numbers of casualties. Once more the arrangements were utterly inadequate. The black ship *Saturnia* was described as 'packed with maggoty wounded'. Two months into the campaign it seemed incredible, to dispassionate observers, that such indifference to the men's suffering could be exhibited. Seemingly intent on exacerbating the problems, the arrival of midsummer brought greater heat. In Cairo temperatures rose to 116 in the shade. The shortages of nurses made it clear that Cairo was a bad choice for medical facilities - it was far too distant

from the coastal port of Alexandria. Both were too distant from Gallipoli. In the heat of the Egyptian interior the flies were intent on bothering every inhabitant of the wards. They were an ever-present plague which made life even more miserable for the wounded.

On 6 August the Gallipoli campaign took a new twist with the landing of two British divisions at Suvla Bay. The objective was to threaten the Turkish

OBJECTIVES FOR THE THIRD BATTLE OF KRITHIA.

The ground-work & trenches are based on a diagram issued with the orders for the battle. That diagram was compiled from aeroplane photographs taken up to the 1st June; & the troops were warned that it was only approximately accurate

REFERENCE
Turkish Trenches.
Wire entanglements.
Probable Turkish Machine guns
Supposed Cmn. Trenches.
Turkish Reserves.
British Trenches
1st Objective.
2nd Objective.
Bde. or Div. Boundaries.
Roads.
Tracks.
Watercourses.

SCALE (APPROX)

Prepared in the Historical Section (Military Branch)

Krithia. (opposite)
The view, looking south westwards, from Krithia towards the site of the Helles landings at the western tip of the Gallipoli Peninsula.

13. May was a bad month for British naval confidence as well. HMS *Goliath* was sunk by a torpedo boat off Helles on the 13th, while at home Lord Fisher resigned two days later.

defences on the south coast of the peninsula which controlled The Narrows. In order to do so the Anafarta Ridge would have to be captured to provide artillery command over the Turkish positions which prevented access to the Sea of Marmara and Constantinople. The Suvla Bay landings had the potential to significantly alter the balance of force on the peninsula but its effectiveness was dulled by poor leadership. The tactical mismanagement of both troops and supplies combined with the devastating heat to which the new arrivals were ill-acclimatised. Initially the landings had been successful and significant numbers were put ashore without opposition. That day the troops passed beyond the salt lake behind the landing beaches and looked up at the Anafarta Hills, the necessary objective, which could be seen glimmering in the haze. Audibly, from the south at ANZAC, and beyond near the peninsula's tip, came the terrible, oppressive and perpetual rumble of artillery. That continuous sound marked the co-ordinated attacks on the Sari Bair Ridge, at Lone Pine and Helles designed to support the Suvla Bay landings. One erudite witness of the events at Suvla Bay was Ellis Ashmead Bartlett, a correspondent whose dispatches revealed the sorry state of the army's growing managerial dislocation.

'August 8th [day three of the landings]. We were up at dawn expecting to see some decisive movement. It was Sunday, and many great British victories have been won on the day of rest. We found to our surprise that it was indeed a day of rest for the army at Suvla, for an almost uncanny peace and calm reigned over the battlefield. I could discern no movement of troops, no sign of any advance, and no khaki figures on the Anafarta Ridge. Not a gun was fired either by the Turks or our warships, and only an occasional rifle shot broke the stillness of this hot August day. I could see our men lying prone in the bush at the foot of the hills, but no attempt to advance; on the contrary, there was rather a retrograde movement. Long lines of stragglers were leaving the front and making their way to the beaches, each festooned with the water-bottles of his comrades. It was evident that water had not been found at the front, and had to be fetched from the beaches. Occasionally small groups advanced short distances but they were soon checked by the enemy's snipers and retired to cover.

The atmosphere became depressing. One could not help feeling that the offensive had suddenly come to a standstill, that the 'punch' had gone out of the attack.

Nevinson and I seized the first opportunity of going ashore and landed at Ghazi Baba. Here we found hundreds of bluejackets and soldiers hastily unloading stores and ammunition. I sat down on some boxes and wrote my first account of the landing - which Delme Radcliffe took back with him to Imbros. I could truthfully cable that we had got ashore successfully, and I gave a description of yesterday's events as they had come under my eye, but I could not mention the acute forebodings which now possessed us. We then set off to explore the country, passing round the long northern arm of Suvla Bay until we came to the sand spit which separates it from the Salt Lake. The scenes en route resembled rather the retreat of a routed army than the advance of a victorious one. Everywhere we encountered stragglers returning from the firing line in a state of pitiful exhaustion from fatigue and thirst, hastening to the beaches to find water at any cost. Many had their tongues hanging from their mouths, blackened with thirst. When they reached the bay they found the water lighters, but no adequate means of filling their bottles. The water was pumped ashore through hose-pipes, but there were no receptacles, and the men were expected to fill bottles a quarter of an inch wide at the spout, from a hose three or four inches in diameter. Naturally, more was wasted than drunk. The hoses were leaking in dozens of places, but I have since learnt that this was due to holes bored by the impatient infantry, who would no longer wait their turn at the spout. The men with whom I spoke seemed dazed and depressed. Not one could tell a coherent story of what had happened, or what was happening at the front. Lack of sleep, thirst, and physical fatigue had killed their interest in the operations. The Anafarta Hills had ceased to be a strategical objective; they were now merely a name, a geographical point in which they were no longer interested. Water and shade alone now counted with men whose objective the day before had been the Narrows and Constantinople...'

Plugge's Plateau. *(opposite)*

On the morning of 25 April the confused landings of the ANZAC troops had brought the majority of the men in the first wave ashore between Ari Burnu and Hell Spit, that is within the confines of what became known as Anzac Cove. No troops landed south of Hell Spit, on what had been designated as the intended landing place or Z Beach, east of which the terrain was less severe and complex. A few of the boats had been drawn onto North Beach under the Sphinx. Due east of Anzac Cove the ground rises onto a broad-topped, steep-sided plateau, named after Lieutenant Colonel Plugge who was the Commanding Officer of the Auckland Battalion.

Johnston's Jolly. *(left)*
This is another place whose colloquial title is an appealing use of soldierly banter and black humour. Within the cramped confines of the Gallipoli campaign senior officers, subordinate officers, non-commissioned officers and other ranks shared the same privations and lived cheek by jowl. Often their blasphemings, personal habits and emotions were known to all. At ANZAC many of the place names derive from the achievements and sayings of officers. This is just one such place. The stretch of ground on the inland aspect of 400 Plateau became known as Johnston's Jolly after Colonel J.H.Johnston (11th West Australian Battalion) who lamented his inability to bring plunging howitzer fire to bear on the Turkish positions here. In his exasperation he had called for a field gun barrage to be laid down on the Turks in an effort to 'jolly them up'. This was much to the dismay of the troops who would now have to endure the counter-battery fire of the Turkish guns.

The following day the sense of despair had become quite tangible.

'August 9th. About midday a new horror was added to this accumulation of tragedies. The heavy shells from the ships started a series of fires which, wafted by a light wind, swept diagonally across the front of Scimitar Hill. Our men ran back to the trenches for cover, and then was seen the ghastly spectacle of many wounded endeavouring to escape from the smoke and flames. The majority were lying in the scrub just beneath the yellow sandy escarpment of Scimitar Hill and their only chance was to crawl out into the open where they would escape the flames, only to be exposed to snipers and shrapnel. Many, alas, sought safety in vain. I watched the flames approaching and the crawling figures disappear amidst dense clouds of black smoke. When the fire passed on little mounds of scorched khaki alone marked the spot where another mismanaged soldier of the King had returned to mother earth. The fire attacked friend and foe alike. It caught the Turks concealed in the scrub. I saw many running like rabbits through the bracken to regain the trenches. While the fire lasted it brought the combat to an end. For both sides it was a question of 'Sauve qui peut'. [Run for your life!]

Turkish trenches at Lone Pine. *(opposite)*
East of Z beach, the ANZACs designated landing site on 25 April, lies the Second Ridge. The central parts of that ridge are broad and were known as 400 Plateau. The eastern limits of the plateau were the objective of the frenzied ANZAC assault on 6 August which coincided with the incompetently managed landings at Suvla Bay to the north. After the Great War these trenches became hidden from view under the burgeoning scrub and pine forest which gradually recaptured all in this area. During the mid-1990s a series of accidental but fortuitous fires removed that vegetation revealing the now shallow trenches and a series of blackened stumps to remind us of what was once a forbidding defensive position overlooking the Aegean waters to the west. The distinctive outline of Gaba Tepe is visible on the shoreline to the top right of the photograph.

Later in the day Nevinson joined me, very exhausted and on the verge of despair. He had been for a walk right round the far side of the lake and his report was most discouraging. 'Our infantry,' he declared, 'are demoralised, weary, and absolutely refuse to advance. The muddle is beyond anything I have ever seen. Never since Nicholson's Neck and Lombard's Kopje have I seen British infantry behave so badly.' Yet there was much to excuse them. Naturally, Nevinson did not have all the facts in his possession at the time.

We made our way back to the beaches amidst hundreds of stragglers who had drifted away from the front simply because they could not stand the pangs of thirst any longer. They were completely done, burnt black, begrimed with dirt, with their tongues blackened, shrivelled, and lolling out of their mouths, their clothes in shreds, and many only in their shirt sleeves. Some, when they reached the sea, rushed into it, even swallowing the salt water. Others waded out to the water-barges, although the distribution had now been arranged on shore. Confusion reigned supreme. No one seemed to know where the headquarters of the different brigades and divisions were to be found. The troops were hunting for water, the staffs were hunting for their troops, and the Turkish snipers were hunting for their prey. Late this evening I ran across Sir Ian Hamilton standing all by himself somewhere near Ghazi Baba. His face was pale and worried, his gaze was directed on the columns of smoke rising leisurely from the smouldering fires along the front of Anafarta. To the Commander-in-Chief it must have been obvious at this hour that his final effort to reach the Narrows had failed.'[14]

In the month following 7 August the flotilla of ships moved 51,867 casualties from the peninsula. Many of those casualties were the product of the Battle of Scimitar Hill at Suvla where four British divisions failed to break through the encircling Turkish positions. The gain, if that is what it can be described as since it had little tactical import in the battle for control of the peninsula's central high ground, was a considerable expansion in the area under the control of British and Empire forces at the now conjoined Suvla - ANZAC position. By 31 August those positions ran through the coastal hills of the Kiretch Tepe Sirt north of Suvla Bay thence southwards across the Suvla plain, between Chocolate Hill and Scimitar Hill. From that low lying position the lines then moved up the foothills of the Sari Bair Ridge across the Rhododendron Spur towards Baby 700 and on to Lone Pine before finally

sinking seawards to Brighton Beach. By late September the casualties amongst the Australian troops in their now rather expanded beachhead had almost reached 20,000, with more than 4,600 men killed. As a proportion of their force these figures were dreadful, but there was enormous pride amongst those troops in their own resilience and toughness.

On each Gallipoli front the men and many of their officers now had little confidence in the High Command. 'I have not met a soldier or sailor with

The Australian Point of View - trenches facing The Nek. *(opposite)*
People who visit the Western Front for the first time are often startled by the proximity of opposing trenches. The front lines were, in a few places, little more than the length of a cricket pitch apart. Behind those lines in France and Belgium each side maintained a great complex of support and reserve trenches with a further multitude of communication trenches and switch lines. Often these elaborate and inter-connected systems went many thousands of yards towards the rear. On the Western Front these lines often ran through drab coal-mining districts as at Loos, or across anonymous pastures such as on the Somme or the lowlands of Flanders.

The situation just above the Aegean Sea on the western side of the Gallipoli peninsula is dramatically different. The front line trenches had no depth of support to their rear at all. Everything was concentrated within a few yards. The compact sandy earth dried out in the summer months to a consistency which made the construction of deep trenches something of a memorial to their creators. Packed close beneath these narrow ridges were a multitude of dug-outs, each housing a tiny cluster of cigarette-smoking, sun-blackened 'Diggers'. Everywhere the ANZACs dug for their lives. Digging was the route to survival.

The heat of the summer afternoon sun on these slopes was intense, yet the men had barely sufficient water to shave. The casual clothing and attitudes of the ANZACs became legendary, stripped to the waist, their hats set at a jaunty angle, utterly indifferent to the norms of deferential behaviour which defined the relationship between other ranks and senior officers in the British recruited units.

The Nek is a phonetic but corrupt description of a narrow stretch of ridge linking Russell's Top and the prominence known as Baby 700. This position therefore lies at a crucial juncture of the First and Second Anzac ridges and it was here that a position of stalemate was reached. An Anzac presence in this location was vital if the whole supply operation to their forward troops on the Second Ridge, across Monash Gully, were not to be enfiladed by unopposed Turkish mortars and machine guns at the head of that valley around The Nek. Baby 700 was the first in a succession of progressively higher hills which led through Battleship Hill to the dominant position of Chunuk Bair. Both sides looked across The Nek at their opponents' trenches which were deep, complex and clearly impenetrable. The Turks looked down on the ANZAC trenches and beyond to the sea, within 1200 metres. The ANZACs were faced by a succession of gullies and ridges stretching interminably into the distance without even the remotest glimpse of the Dardanelles, the initial object of their presence here.

14. Ellis Ashmead Bartlett, *The Uncensored Dardanelles*, pub: Hutchinson.

confidence in Ian Hamilton. They do not see the reasons for these frontal attacks on prepared death traps.'

The men settled to the business of preserving themselves. A sense of inevitable and interminable stress settled over the battlefields.

Early in October Lord Kitchener requested information from Hamilton about the possible human cost of an evacuation. Hamilton's terse reply was an estimate of 50% casualties. Within 24 hours he was removed from the command of the Gallipoli forces and replaced by General Sir Charles Monro whose inspection of the peninsula during the final three days of October 1915 led him to recommend withdrawal of all forces. However, politicians were unable to decide the issue quickly; any withdrawal would be a tacit

The movement of supplies and the evacuation of casualties required a superhuman effort in appalling conditions once autumnal rains set in.

admission of failure, even defeat. To clarify the situation Kitchener himself came to Gallipoli on 4 November to see what could be salvaged. Within twelve days Kitchener had inspected the ground and concluded, as had Monro, that evacuation was inevitable. Unlike Monro, Kitchener felt that it was necessary, in order to retain some degree of dignity, to maintain the beachhead at Helles. The end of November held yet another twist in the tail of this desperate story. Violent storms beset the peninsula. Water cascaded down the trenches and unprotected gullies causing widespread flooding and costing the lives of 300 men. The floods were followed by blizzards and freezing weather conditions which caused 13,000 cases of frostbite.

On 7 December the British cabinet agreed to Kitchener's proposal for the withdrawal of all forces except those at Helles. By 11 December the full panoply of British and Empire forces' casualties on the peninsula had become apparent.

Ocean Beach - the area of the allied assault up the slopes towards Chunuk Bair and Koja Chemen Tepe on the Sari Bair Ridge. (opposite)

The Sari Bair ridge looks north-westwards across the open space of the Suvla plain. For that landing, on 6 August, to threaten the Turkish forces' ability to hold onto the Gallipoli peninsula it was necessary to capture the dominant Sari Bair positions whose observation utterly controlled this area. Between The Nek and the highest ground of the ridge, Koja Chemen Tepe, the land was described by Hamilton as '...worse than the Khyber Pass'. In co-operation with the Suvla landings, the New Zealanders made a remarkable and astonishingly brave assault on Sari Bair. That attack was launched in the late afternoon of 6 August, but was beset by severe tactical difficulties. Throughout the dark night hours units stumbled lost in the many gullies losing casualties to the numerous Turkish snipers who caused chaos among their opponents. The following morning the advance was still below the crest of the Sari Bair Ridge. Nevertheless, the New Zealand Canterbury and Wellington battalions with troops from the 4th Australian Brigade made some further progress. On the morning of the 8th the New Zealanders took Chunuk Bair. The following day, the 1/6th Battalion, Gurkha Rifles, took Hill Q, between Chunuk Bair and Koja Chemen Tepe. The Dardanelles were enticingly in sight.

That, however, was as far as this initiative went. Within seconds shells began to burst around the Gurkhas. Which side fired those shells has been a matter of controversy for decades. Some believed them to have been shells fired mistakenly by the Royal Navy. Whoever was responsible it utterly quashed the Gurkhas' progress. The next day, 10 August, the Turkish forces, under the inspirational leadership of Mustafa Kemal, made a crushing counterattack.

This effectively sounded the end of the Gallipoli campaign. Failure to capture the Sari Bair Ridge meant that the British forces now trapped at Suvla would be impotent to threaten the Turkish stranglehold on the peninsula. The ANZAC forces were still locked within their oppressive confines beneath the same uplands.

'In seven months more than 25,000 men had perished; 75,000 were wounded, while over 12,000 were missing. Casualties nearly twice the number of the force which landed on April 25th...over 96,000 cases had been admitted to hospital. The chief causes, dysentery and para-typhoid.'

The final irony of the Gallipoli campaign was that the enforced evacuation was the most successful part of it. By 18 December final preparations had been made and half of the Suvla and ANZAC garrisons were taken off. Two days later, on December 20, an evacuation of the remaining men was mounted. The Turkish troops were completely deceived. Almost three weeks later, by the night of 8/9 January 1916, the evacuation of the British troops

This photograph captures the moment when officers and men steel themselves to advance across No Man's Land in the summer heat at Gallipoli.

from Sedd-el-Bahr and the Helles tip of the peninsula was completed. Again the process was undertaken without mishap - just one casualty.

Throughout the campaign as a whole the expedition to Gallipoli soaked up 410,000 British and Empire troops along with 79,000 French troops. In total there were 213,980 British and Empire casualties. Of these more than 145,000 were due to sickness with 50,000 cases of dysentery, diarrhoea and enteric fever stemming from the impossibility of maintaining sanitary conditions and hygienic food preparation facilities. These were casualties that could be ill-afforded. Gallipoli had become an expensive and unnecessary side-show. One eminent historian, John Terraine, concluded that;

'For Britain Gallipoli held another, even more serious meaning: this was the last attempt in British history to exercise absolute naval supremacy in the traditional manner. Since the British Empire was founded upon naval might, one may say that the Gallipoli failure marked the beginning of the end of that Empire.'[15]

---

15. Terraine, *White Heat - The New Warfare* 1914 - 1918, Leo Cooper.

Suvla Bay - the view from Nibrunesi Point towards Suvla. *(opposite)*
Many visitors have been moved by the poetic beauty of Suvla Bay and its stark, brilliant, open vista. It is, possibly, the most instantly appealing of Gallipoli's many and varied landscapes.

'From Chunuk Bair when the mist is thin there is a sparkling view north across the whole area with the Salt Lake, when it is dry, shimmering diamond white in the sun. Around it yellow fields and green trees are scattered loosely across the lush plain, while, beyond, a harsh black line of hills scours the horizon. To the west the violet blue waters of the bay are kept deathly still, without a tremor of movement passing across them, by an embracing ring of land that reaches out into the Aegean Sea. Along the margin of the bay a long, hot beach of powdery sand runs for several miles without a person on it. It is hard to imagine a more beautiful place.'

The landings at Suvla Bay, on the night of 6/7 August were destined to be a race against both time and the arrival of Turkish forces from Bulair. The Corps Commander, charged with impressing the need for vigorous and speedy advance, was Sir Frederick Stopford and from the start he proved to be a poor choice, working to minimise the risks rather than to maximise the impact of his Corps' attacks upon the high ground of the surrounding hills. It was anticipated that the advance of Stopford's Corps would be undertaken concomitantly with an ANZAC assault upon the highest ground of the Sari Bair positions.

Having secured the beaches and the Suvla Bay headlands, an advance inland would then take Yilghin Burnu and Ismail Oglu Tepe before securing a footing on the Tekke Tepe Ridge before crossing the Anafarta valley to assault the summit of Koja Chemen Tepe. Such an outflanking advance would then threaten the Turkish positions overlooking ANZAC and give British control over the highest ground on the Gallipoli peninsula.

An act of compassion at Pine Ridge. (left)
A Turkish Mehmet carries a wounded Australian Officer. The gesture's sympathy, simplicity and honourable intent is timeless.

Throughout the Gallipoli campaign the relationship between the soldiers of both belligerents was not one of disdain or thoughtless animosity. It was soon realised, by the fiery civilians who made up the bulk of the Australian and New Zealand Corps, that the Turkish troops were brave, disciplined and committed. At ANZAC that commitment to the cause of Turkish sovereignty was tested to the very limits. Here a sequence of Turkish counter-attacks led many thousands of young soldiers to their deaths at the hands of desperate riflemen clinging tenaciously to their precarious positions around The Nek and Quinn's post. Throughout the Gallipoli campaign the ANZACs fought with their backs to the sea. Failure to hold the Turkish counter-attacks was therefore not an option. Yet within the intense fighting which such a situation generated there was compassion. Prisoners were treated well by their opponents. This statue on Pine Ridge symbolises that respect for humanity during a recorded incident when a Turkish soldier carried this officer back to the ANZAC lines for treatment.

The ANZAC memorial and cemetery at Lone Pine. (opposite)
This location was named after a lone pine tree, visible during the first months of the campaign, on the south-eastern limits of 400 Plateau. Initially captured by the ANZACs' it was recaptured on the evening of the 26th by a Turkish counter-attack. It was again captured by the Australians during the frenzied and desperate attack which took place at 5.30 pm on 6 August, being subsequently held as a front line position until the evacuation. Here 1,167 graves are placed in the cemetery, whilst the memorial records the names of 4,932 men who have no known grave, of whom 4,233 are ANZACs.

To this place many young Australians and New Zealanders are inevitably drawn. The memorial, and the event which it commemorates, draws a sentimental and conclusive dividing line across the relationship between Britain and her antipodean Empire partners. The strength of that sentiment is derived in full from the terrible severity of fighting here at Lone Pine in the six days after the assault here on 6 August 1915. Its lonely isolation serves to remind visitors that many thousands came here from the other side of the planet, never to return. But as an introduction to the Gallipoli campaign the memorial gives a false impression - some people leave here in the belief that Australia bore the greatest cost of the Gallipoli campaign. They should go to the French cemetery and ossuaries near Morto Bay at the tip of the peninsula. It contains 2340 identified graves and five ossuaries containing the remains of 12,000 bodies. Yet in the broad sweep of France's part in the Great War the Gallipoli campaign is a mere footnote. Gallipoli therefore merits limited reference in French historiography which rightly concentrates on a far more terrible journey through four years of occupation and nightmare along the Western Front.

The Memorial to Mustafa Kemal.

High on Chunuk Bair there stand two remarkable memorials. One is to those men who came 'from the uttermost ends of the earth', the New Zealanders, who once captured and held this ridge for two days. The other is to Mustafa Kemal Pasha. Kemal was a nickname which Mustafa incorporated into his own to lend distinction. It means 'perfectionist'. Kemal was no friend to Enver Pasha who, during the years before the war, seemed to do all in his considerable power to limit the scope of Kemal's career. Unlike Enver Pasha, Kemal was not an enthusiast for the German mission which came in late 1913, nor for the links which led to Turkey's entrance into war as a belligerent on the side of the Central Powers. But that war was to shape Kemal's destiny. After the war Enver Pasha was consigned to ignominy. Kemal was to become renowned as 'Ataturk', the father of the Turkish nation.

Kemal was born in Salonika in northern Greece. At the time of his birth Greece was still administered as a part of the Ottoman Empire and Kemal's family were part of that extended bureaucracy. In the turbulent years before the Great War Kemal fought with distinction in a succession of losing battles during the Italo-Turkish war of 1911-12 and subsequent Balkan Wars. By 1913, with the rank of Lieutenant Colonel, Kemal was consigned to the role of Military Attaché at Sofia, capital city of Bulgaria. There he was a deeply troubled man. 1915 saw Kemal placed by Liman von Sanders as head of the 19th Division, the reserve division on the Gallipoli peninsula. The British Official History makes plain Kemal's enormous contribution to the successful Turkish campaign at Gallipoli and the ultimate defeat of the invading forces:

'It was that officer's ready grip of the situation on the 25th April which was primarily responsible for the failure of the Anzac corps to gain its objectives on the first day of the landing. It was his vigorous action on the 9th August, when entrusted at a moment's notice with the command of the northern zone, that checked and defeated the long-delayed advance of the IX Corps. And, twenty-four hours later, following a personal reconnaissance, it was his brilliant counter-attack at Chunuk Bair which placed the Turks in undisputed possession of the main Sari Bair ridge. Seldom in history can the exertions of a single divisional commander have exercised, on three separate occasions, so profound an influence not only on the course of a battle, but perhaps on the fate of a campaign and even the destiny of a nation.'

After the war Kemal led the uprising against the Treaty of Sevres in 1923, drove out the Greeks in the War of Liberation and reclaimed Gallipoli along with Turkey's other European territory. From there Kemal reshaped every political structure to create a modern secular state. This was the moment when Kemal added the epithet Ataturk to his name. It was Kemal's reforms which liberated Turkish women who were democratised with the vote in 1934, just five years after their counterparts in Britain. That was the settling of a debt because Mustafa Kemal knew full well what a central role had been played by women in the maintenance of agricultural production during the war years when the countryside was denuded of men called to fight at Gallipoli and elsewhere. Today Ataturk's picture appears in every institution across the Republic. His was and is an enduring reputation and imagery. It was created here at Gallipoli where Allied forces played their unintentional part in forging Turkey's place in the modern world.

CHAPTER THREE

SOMME 1

Here Comes Kitchener's Army

The year 1916 is a seminal moment in the Great War's history. This was the year of Verdun, the Somme and the Brusilov Offensive. Each would drain the German army of a massive slice of its human reserves. Germany's potential to replace her losses was hugely eroded by its aberrant willingness to engage in battles of attrition. The scope and intensity of the fighting brought home, to politicians and influential elites across Europe, the fact that this was total and extended war requiring the mobilisation of all of each combatant nation's resources. Germany's failure to achieve a quick victory by 1915 gradually gave rise to the feeling in France, Britain and even Russia that it might be possible to achieve victory rather than a compromise peace. But once the huge costs of 1916 had been realised it was too late to turn back; any compromise was an admission of failure.

The start of 1916 was a period of great optimism in the minds of Kitchener's soldiers. The appearance of a British army 50 divisions strong 'was as surprising to the Germans as it was remarkable to the British themselves'[1]. But this was an army whose potential was, in large part,

destined to be shattered within six months of its arrival in France. Today, more than eighty years on, nothing exerts a more powerful or sentimental pull upon popular conceptions of the Great War than the Battles of the Somme. Fought between 1 July and mid-November 1916 it is still the events on that fateful first summer morning, 1 July 1916, which fascinate and repel in equal measure. In the decades that I have known of these events I have never tired of their terrible, grim, inspiring message.

Where Gallipoli had revealed the way in which modern battle created casualties in numbers which overwhelmed the forward and surgical facilities, as well as the medical evacuation, transport and hospitalisation services, the Battle of the Somme generated a social shock which rocked the very fabric of British society. There always have been communities, within our society, which have lived with the danger of armed conflict. Garrison towns such as Portsmouth or Aldershot have invariably known this. But the Somme brought concentrations of loss to almost every corner of the country, often to communities whose men had volunteered together into units known

1. *Passchendaele in Perspective*, Ed P.Liddle, Pen & Sword Books Ltd, 1997.

A Typical Battalion of Kitchener's New Armies. This is one of the Salford Pals Battalions in training at Conway.

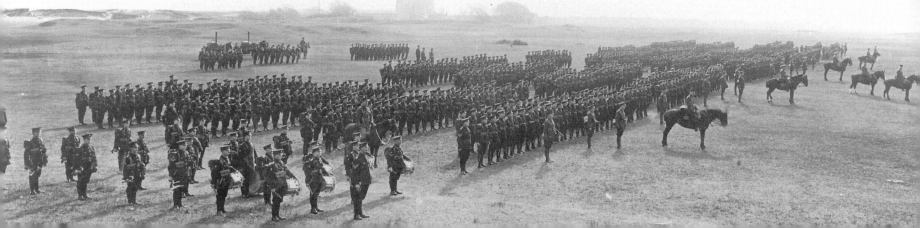

Hebuterne, Fonquevillers and Gommecourt.

Hebuterne and Fonquevillers lay just behind the British front line positions at the northern end of the Somme battlefield. To the east of both villages lay Gommecourt which was to be the objective of a subsidiary offensive assault made by two divisions, the 46th and the 56th on the morning of 1st July. The 56th (1st London T.F.) were an experienced Territorial unit comprising battalions from the capital city.

The assault on Gommecourt would be a diversion to draw German attention from the greater part of the British effort to be made two miles further south, along a twelve mile frontage between Serre and Montauban. Observation was critical and the British army had prepared concrete OPs to protect their Forward Observation Officers. The artillery duel between both armies was particularly severe in this area before the attack. Nevertheless, most German soldiers had survived in the many deep dug-outs in the area. When the assault was made at 7.30 am the artillery observers saw quickly that, whilst the 56th Division's advance was successful, that of the 46th was repulsed.

The photograph above shows No Man's Land in front of the 56th Division's positions, facing the south-western side of Gommecourt Park. Once the 56th Division had moved forward the area was thickly strewn with dead and severely wounded men. German machine gun and artillery fire remained so intense that it proved impossible to get reinforcements forward to those units fighting within the German trenches south of Gommecourt. The expenditure of munitions during the assault of 1st July 1916, by soldiers of both sides, was phenomenal. A division would normally have prepared forward 'dumps' of small arms ammunition amounting to 6,000,000 rounds. Across that divisional frontage some 66,000 grenades would be available to the infantry. The artillery, firing a multiplicity of different calibre high explosive and shrapnel shells had expended thousands of shells on every area of the German trench network. A significant number of the British shells proved to be 'duds' - some shell types suffered a 30% failure rate. Troops advancing often commentated later on the numbers of unexploded shells which were strewn over the battlefield. Many are still collected today by the farmers in this area, a seemingly never ending 'Iron Harvest'. At Gommecourt the casualties suffered by the 46th and 56th Divisions were appalling. 80% amongst two Sherwood Forester battalions attacking on the north-west of Gommecourt. But amongst the 56th Division the casualties were even more extensive.

Today Gommecourt's sedate tranquillity is unruffled by the terrible history which once unfolded within its composed confines. In my experience a number of Somme villages have never been able to shake off the memory of an ugly and pernicious evil which once stalked their wreckage. Gommecourt has no such legacy and the village and its surrounding agrarian scene are only infrequently visited by people seeking to understand the lessons of war today.

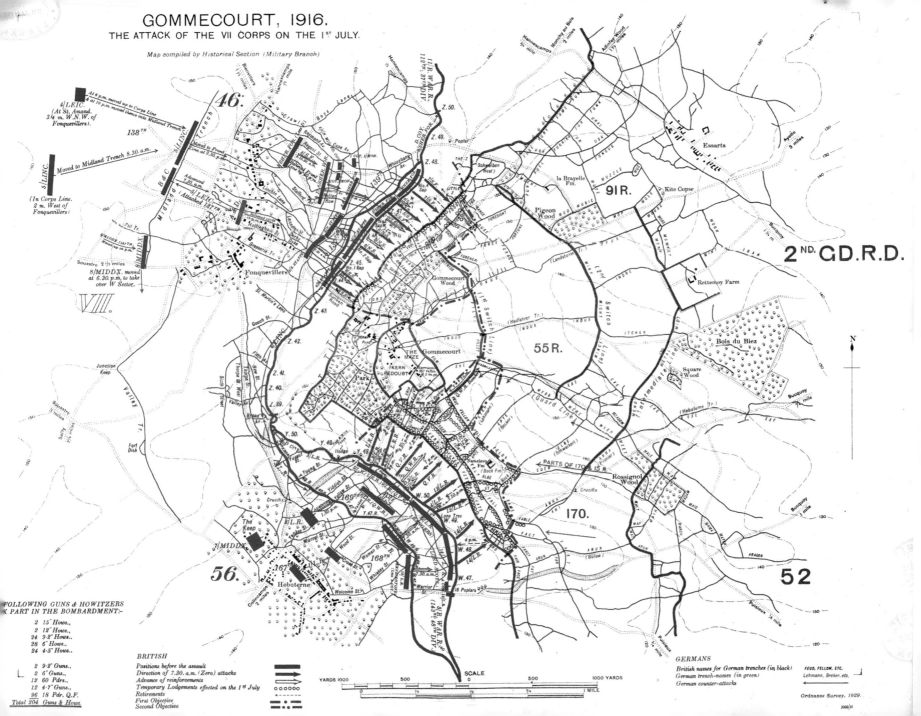

GOMMECOURT, 1916.
THE ATTACK OF THE VII CORPS ON THE 1ST JULY.

Map compiled by Historical Section (Military Branch)

FOLLOWING GUNS & HOWITZERS
K PART IN THE BOMBARDMENT:-

2 15" Hows.,
2 12" Hows.,
24 9·2" Hows.,
28 6" Hows.,
24 4·5" Hows.,

2 9·2" Guns.,
2 6" Guns.,
12 60 Pdrs.,
12 4·7" Guns.,
96 18 Pdr. Q.F.

Total 204 Guns & Hows.

BRITISH
Positions before the assault
Direction of 7.30. a.m. (Zero) attacks
Advance of reinforcements
Temporary Lodgements effected on the 1st July
Retirements
First Objective
Second Objective

GERMANS
British names for German trenches (in black)
German trench-names (in green)
German counter-attacks

FEUD, FELLOW, ETC.
Lehmann, Becker, etc.

SCALE
YARDS 1000   500   0   500   1000 YARDS

Ordnance Survey, 1929.

2000/31

colloquially by their home town or occupation's name, the Tyneside Commercials, Hull Tradesmen, Glasgow Tramways, Belfast Young Citizens or the Salford Pals. The history of Kitchener's New Army and the town of Albert are therefore joined umbilically. It is true that Albert's shattered dust-laden streets stood watching for four long years of war as generations of young men, French, British, Australian and German, marched through here, but the nadir of Albert's notoriety was its forbidding place in 1916's history when the town became the very hub of the British effort during the Battles of the Somme. It was the sheer scale of the Somme's casualty figures, concentrated within Kitchener's New Army, which hurt so deeply.

Here we have a focal point through which all troops passed. Almost every British Tommy and Empire soldier who survived on the Western Front for any length of time came here. If he cared to look up into the blackness of night the distant flickerings of shell fall and flares on the ridges could be seen, incessantly. The necessary movements of troops were invariably undertaken in darkness. Throughout those nocturnal hours men could hear the rumble of artillery and the occasional, seemingly innocent, distant rattle of machine-gun fire. In the perverse world of warfare, where observation was everything, the night time was when things happened, gun teams moved, rations brought forward, units relieved. Battalions of soldiers on the move marched apprehensively beneath the crumbling tower of the basilica with its Madonna and Child – carefully propped with scaffolds and wires by British engineers in case the rumour, that were the 'Golden Virgin' to fall the war would end, proved true! [2]

The transfixing sentiment of the first day of the battle, 1 July 1916, is linked to our image of those stoical lines of disciplined volunteers marching forward, their rifles at the slope, waiting for the sound of unseen machine guns whose grim crackle, tak, tak, tak would reap a terrible toll. In truth the machine gun was by no means the most lethal weapon. That accolade was held by the artillery. Almost 60% of British casualties on the Somme were caused by shelling. Its impact was the tear a man to pieces. Various forms of shells sought men on the battlefield during attacks, within his trenches and dugouts in quieter times, in his billets and rest areas to the rear, on the march between any location. It terrified and shocked all who knew it. Men waited for years in the certainty that one shell would have their number on it. On the Somme only 39.98% of the casualties came from the bullet.

✦ ✦ ✦

Since the first weeks of August 1914 the Secretary of State for War, Lord Kitchener, had made it his business to inspire the recruitment of volunteers. Throughout the months of late 1914 and early 1915 he had tapped a seemingly overwhelming tide of patriotic fervour. The result was an army brimful of quality, burnished with a sense of belief and identity. They were, as many have since remarked, the finest men that Britain had ever fielded as an army. But they were also naive. Their training had been marked by equipment shortages. In the context of an already well established stalemate in France their sense of optimism was misplaced. Most of Kitchener's divisions travelled to France in the late autumn of 1915. It was unlikely that any massive deployment of these soldiers could stand a chance of effectively turning the course of the war. Yet that is what was expected of them. And that is what the men expected to achieve through their participation in 'The Great Push'.

The scale and duration of the Somme battles, nearly five months, made almost all previous military engagements seem relatively small by comparison. The sense of purpose was made all the more intense by parallel events at Verdun where French and German forces were locked in a near suicidal struggle throughout the spring and early summer months of 1916. That attritional battle had begun on 21 February and was still raging as the bombardment of German positions before the Battle of the Somme commenced. Put simply, it was imperative that the French be relieved by a major demonstration of British resolve. Whilst the initial Allied planning suggested that the great thrust would be undertaken as a joint initiative

---

2. It did so in 1918, brought down by British artillery fire after that year's German spring offensives captured the town.

astride the River Somme, the reality became a dwindling of French participation with the resultant switch of emphasis northwards in the direction of the British positions which lay both to the north and south of the Roman road running between the towns of Albert and Bapaume. The British component of the battles ought therefore to be thought of, more appropriately, as the Battle of the Ancre - itself a tributary of the Somme - which flows through Albert.

Throughout these battles the engagement of whole communities brought fresh anguish to the traditional sense of outrage which accompanies all war. In the great industrial and commercial towns and cities men who formed the very backbone of whole communities had enlisted en masse. Their decimation in battle meant a concentration of grief never seen in Britain, before or since. Local newspapers from Salford to Swansea, Glasgow to Greenwich and many between were overwhelmed by thousands of tragic biographical entries recording the passage of life. Whole towns were stunned and devastated by the Somme's consequences.

On 1 July 1916 the Battle of the Somme began. The assault followed an imposing, week-long, artillery bombardment of the German positions, during which 1,627,824 shells of various calibres had been fired. The battle was engaged on a front twenty-five miles in width. Roughly half of that width was assaulted by British troops, the remainder by the French army on their right. The British sector had already been, during 1914 and 1915, the scene of intense fighting involving the French, before British troops took over this sector later that year. By late June 1916 the small village of Serre marked the topographical start of the major and continuous British struggles which unfolded throughout the remainder of that terrible year. Like the diversionary assaults at Gommecourt, two miles to the north, the British soldiers who went forward at Serre were handicapped by having an unprotected left flank. The Division which attacked on 1 July at Serre, the 31st, was composed principally of men from the north of England, Pals units from Hull, Leeds, Bradford, Accrington, Sheffield and Barnsley. In military terms the 31st were not hardened - as yet untried in battle.

The two divisions deployed at Serre were entrusted with different tasks. The 31st were to advance before forming a defensive position facing north. Success in that enterprise would mean that the division on their right, the 4th Division, would not suffer from enfilade fire as they moved across the Redan Ridge south of Serre. Today Serre village is an unprepossessing place with little to remind visitors of what savagery it has witnessed. Only by walking

away from the village, down the lane which leads towards where the Pals were decimated in front of Matthew, Mark, Luke and John Copse can you see the real tragedy which was the 1st of July 1916. The legacy of that tragedy is forever encapsulated in a sequence of deeply moving cemeteries, added to without constraint during the summer and autumnal months of 1916.

Although he was not a participant in the events at Serre, Siegfried Sassoon, writing from the tortured perspective of a brilliant and brave officer, captured the last moments of those Pals.

Do you remember that hour of din before the attack -
And the anger, the blind compassion that seized and shook you then
As you peered at the doomed and haggard faces of your men?
Do you remember the stretcher-cases lurching back
With dying eyes and lolling heads - those ashen-grey
Masks of the lads who once were keen and kind and gay?

[A fragment of Aftermath by Siegfried Sassoon.]

These first attacks on 1 July 1916, undertaken under the brilliant sunshine of a blisteringly hot morning, will forever be regarded as an act of astonishing

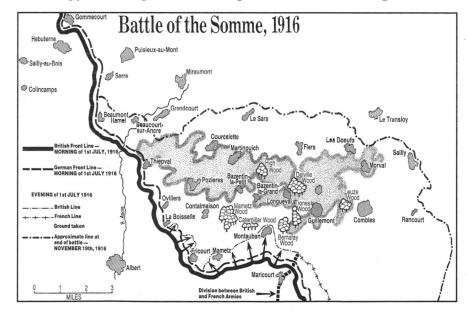

Battle of the Somme, 1916

bravery and ultimate folly by succeeding generations. Eye-witness accounts speak eloquently of the incredible steadfastness and bravery required of each participant.

'There was neither confusion nor haste when the signal came. The men clambered out from the trenches into the metal-swept open ground, and in a line dead straight and true made steadily forward - as if on parade - for the enemy. Men fell rapidly under the deadly fire, but the remainder swept on, and shortly the second and third lines came over to fill up the gaps.' [Unknown soldier quoted in: *Leeds Pals*. Milner. pp141.]

'I dropped myself in a shell-hole...the memory's terrible...I got in the shell hole and that's where I stuck. I'd a spot on my arm it was just cut and a bullet in through the top of my leg. I was unconscious, laid in that trench and that's where I laid the whole day. I could see the bodies going up in the air. A terrible sight, a sight that I'll never forget, and the ground was just like an upheaval, one mass of flame everywhere.' [15/339 Private Morrison Fleming, D Company, *Leeds Pals*. Quoted in Milner. pp 142.]

To the south-west of Serre and the Redan ridge two villages faced each other across No Man's Land. Their names are redolent of the whole British campaign here during 1916. To the west lies Auchonvillers, just behind the British lines and home to numerous command posts and forward medical units. Like Fonquevillers to the north its buildings were utterly devastated by shellfire, but its numerous cellars gave subterranean shelter and comfort to the men who passed through. To the east was Beaumont Hamel. Lying in a valley which runs parallel to the front lines it completely dominated the route which the 29th Division would have to take if they were to advance here. The village and nearby embankments provided numerous ideal sites for deep infantry shelters which the German army had constructed in abundance here.

Railway Hollow Cemetery at Serrre (opposite)

Almost every visitor who knows the quiet simplicity of this emotive spot returns. It is an unforgettable part of the 1916 Somme battlefield. It was from trenches in this place that the 31st Division, sometimes later cruelly and inappropriately referred to as the 'Thirty Worst', attacked Serre on the morning of 1July 1916. The men were a defining selection of Pals units from Yorkshire and Lancashire.

Today the atmosphere is serene and many personal and communal memorials can be found within a short distance of this place. Numerous school parties come here in search of understanding. More effectively than any other place, this quiet combination of small cemeteries, massively significant history and fascinating topography seems to stimulate the minds of teachers. When given inspirationally the lessons here provide a lifetime of insight into the nature of humanity. I can never forget the poetry read with such equanimity, poise and meaning by colleagues and students here. As the sun goes down this is a sublime place to dwell on the words of Owen, Sassoon and Binyon.

No Man's Land here at Serre was an evil place to be trapped on the morning of 1 July 1916. Men attempting, amongst the terrible sounds and sights of battle, to cross this area were enfiladed from both north and south that morning. From the north that fire was coming from the German trenches between Gommecourt and Serre which were not subject to a British assault. From the south it came from a sequence of immensely strong German trenches concentrated in an area known as 'The Quadrilateral'. Today that is the site of Serre Road No 2 cemetery. From in front it came from hundreds of German soldiers who stood confidently on their front line positions, often fully visible to all, firing rifles and numerous machine guns at the advancing waves of Tommies.

The French Cemetery at Serre seems rather out of sequence. British cemeteries dominate the landscape here but disguise the fact that Britain's Army was a late arrival in this fiercely contested corner of France. The burial grounds of British servicemen are scattered across the Serre landscape in a seemingly profligate manner. Visitors from Britain and Commonwealth countries are present here every day of the year – yet the French cemetery, into which many Gallic graves from the 1914-15 fighting near to here were concentrated, often goes unseen and unvisited.

Just behind the British front lines facing Beaumont Hamel was a position known to the troops as 'White City'. Its chalk spoil thrown up by troops digging a complex of defences here could be seen for miles - hence the name. Overlooking the road leading into Beaumont Hamel the official cinematographer, Geoffrey Malins, had set up his camera to record the events here, especially the imminent and rather premature detonation of a mine under Hawthorn Ridge. Malins' incredible film of the detonation of that mine is one of the enduring images of the Great War.

The crater on Hawthorn Ridge was the result of the explosion of 40,000 pounds (18,000 kg.) of ammonal which had been placed under the German strongpoint which dominated the ridge. That mine was prepared by the 252nd Tunnelling Company of the Royal Engineers. It was detonated at 7.20 am and the ten minutes of advance warning which this gave to the German defences were significant. It was the 2nd Royal Fusiliers whose task it was to occupy the crater, but they were unable to get to its eastern side. Everywhere in the vicinity the German machine gunners and riflemen had rushed into forward positions, forewarned by the obvious preparation which had been preceeding for a week, now knowing of the imminence of the assault which was confirmed by the mine's detonation.

George Ashurst, a bomber with the 1st LFs, was in the vicinity of Lanwick Street when the attack started at 7.30. He passed through the carnage of battle as he pressed forward to the Sunken Lane north of the crater.

'We set our teeth; we seemed to say to ourselves all in a moment, 'To hell with life', and as the shout of our comrades in the front line leaping over the top reached us above the din of battle, we bent low in the trench and moved forward. Fritz's shells were screaming down on us fast now; huge black shrapnel shells seemed to burst on top of us. Shouts of pain and calls for help could be heard on all sides; as we stepped forward we stepped over mortally wounded men who tried to grab our legs as we passed them, or we squeezed to one side of the trench while wounded men struggled by us anxious to get gaping wounds dressed and reach the safety of the dugouts in the rear. Men uttered terrible curses even as they lay dying from terrible wounds, and others sat at the bottom of the trench shaking and shouting, not wounded but unable to bear the noise, the smell and the horrible sights.'

Bearing a charmed life, Ashurst crossed the shell-torn British front line trench and struggled forward to the Sunken Road.

'Miraculously, I breathlessly reached the Sunken Road, practically leaping the last yard or two, and almost diving into its shelter. Picking myself up, and looking around, my God, what a sight! The whole of the road was strewn with dead and dying men. Some were talking deliriously, others calling for help and asking for water.'

Another location, south-west of Beaumont Hamel and north of Hamel village, was the scene of a further heart-rending military tragedy this day. As elsewhere on much of the Somme battlefront, a significant part of the German barbed wire, protecting their trenches, had not been swept away by British shellfire. In the gaps between wire men bunched together in their attempts to get forward and became easy prey to the German machine gunners. In front of Beaumont Hamel all the first wave of attacks at 7.30 am ground to a halt. Rumour and inaccurate observation, often clouded by the heat and dust of battle, meant that divisional commanders had little accurate idea of what was

This photograph shows the moment of detonation when the British mine under Hawthorn Ridge destroyed German positions in front of Beaumont Hamel. The moment was captured by Geoffrey Malins' camera from his postion at the White City.

happening as their troops either made progress or were swallowed into the abyss of growing casualty figures. Even though here at Beaumont Hamel there was little progress, General de Lisle had been told, erroneously, that the 87th Brigade were moving forward in force. Seeking to exploit that seemingly advantageous situation de Lisle ordered the Reserve Brigade, the 88th, to move its two leading battalions forward.

On the right of the 88th Brigade were the 1st Essex battalion, on the left the Newfoundland Regiment.

'There would be no artillery support; but they would be covered by a barrage from the 88th Machine Gun Company. At 9.5 a.m only the 1st Newfoundland Regiment, the left battalion, advanced over the open. It did so independently by brigade orders, as the start of the 1st Essex on its right had been delayed by the complete congestion of the trenches with the bodies of dead and dying, in places piled one on the other, through which it was attempting to move.

No sooner had this isolated and doomed attack of the Newfoundlanders left cover than their ranks were swept with bullets from the German position around Y Ravine. Dropping dead and wounded, as an artillery observer reported, at every yard, nevertheless the battalion pressed on, never faltering. The majority of the men were hit before they had gone much beyond the British wire, but some got across No Man's Land and actually reached the German trench and disappeared into it before they were finally shot down. The battalion suffered over seven hundred casualties, and was literally annihilated, losing every one of its officers, actually three more than the number it should have taken into action. The 1st Essex coming up later, also suffered very heavily as soon as it left the front trenches, both from artillery on the right and machine-gun fire, particularly on the left. The fourth company was held back. Nevertheless, here too a few men reached the German position before they were killed. The survivors of both battalions remained lying out in No Man's Land.'

[Source. Military Operations. France and Belgium. 1916. Vol. 1. pp 436.]

Casualties amongst the 29th Division this day amounted to 223 officers and 5,017 other ranks. Most battalions engaged had more than 400 casualties. Six battalions, the 2nd Royal Fusiliers, 16th Middlesex, 1st King's Own Scottish Borderers, 1st Inniskilling Fusiliers, 1st Border Regiment and the Newfoundland Regiment had more than 500 casualties. Of these the highest figure was borne by the Newfoundlanders whose losses amounted to 710 of all ranks. It was the worst loss amongst a single British Army battalion in any day's fighting throughout the entirety of the Great War.

Further south, on the opposite bank of the River Ancre, lay the key to the northern segment of the British effort on 1 July 1916. Observation from the broad shoulders of the Thiepval ridge dominated the ground to the north across the River Ancre. From here German observers could see past Serre towards Gommecourt with ease. In the context of the opening day of the Battle of the Somme these slopes were to be the most formidable obstacle to success. Astride the Ancre it was the Ulstermen of the 36th Division who would attack the seemingly impregnable Schwaben Redoubt. The village itself would be assaulted by the Salford Pals and the Tyneside Commercials of 32nd Division. Those Tyneside Commercials, shipping clerks, warehousemen, salesmen and travellers before the war, were caught in overwhelmingly heavy fire. Opposite them, just a hundred yards above, amidst the trenches which surrounded Thiepval, the German troops taunted the Tynesiders. So confident were the German troops that they could be seen, standing above the parapet

'When the barrage lifted A and B Coys moved forward in waves and were instantly fired upon by Enemy's M.G and snipers. The enemy stood upon their parapet and waved to our men to come on and picked them off with rifle fire. The Enemy's fire was so intense that the advance was checked and the waves, or what was left of them, were forced to lie down. On observing this, C Coy, the support Coy, moved out to reinforce the front line, losing a great number of men in doing so ..... orders were given for D Coy, the reserve Coy, to advance. Getting over the parapet the first Platoon lost a great number of men and the remainder of the Coy was ordered to 'stand fast' and hold the line.'

[Source. 16th Northumberland Fusiliers' War Diary. Public Record Office.]

During this first day of battle the Ulstermen created a broad inroad into the German positions, sweeping across the Pope's Nose[3], past the Schwaben Redoubt and penetrating to the German main Second Positions between Grandcourt and Mouquet farm.

During this courageous advance hundreds of prisoners were sent back, many of whom were glad of the chance to outpace their escorts across the terrors of the battlefield and into the anticipated sanctuary of Thiepval Wood! In the heat of the battle these German prisoners stood little chance. The War

---

3. Adjacent to the site of the Ulster Tower.

Diary of the 10th Inniskilling Fusiliers is vivid in its description of what happened to the first clutches of captured men.

'Enemy prisoners now began to come in, most of them having evidently been concealed in deep dug-outs in the German support trench which runs close behind their front trench. They seemed for the most part dazed and bewildered by the fury of our bombardment and were only too glad to surrender and throw down their arms. They were sent back under escort to our trenches - about 16 prisoners to each escorting soldier. The first batches of these prisoners were so anxious to reach the shelter of our trenches that they outstripped their escort in the dash across the open and meeting our reinforcing lines coming forward were bayoneted by them in the heat of the moment. Some reached our trenches and were there hunted by the few of our men remaining in our front line....'

[Source. 10th Inniskilling Fusiliers' War Diary. Public Record Office.]

This was almost predictable since the 'reinforcing lines' were from the 11th Royal Inniskilling Fusiliers, a battalion which had already suffered heavy casualties from the machine guns in Schwaben and Thiepval which now had the range of the Ulster units crossing No Man's Land.

Tragically the Ulstermen's advance through this devastating scene was compromised by the inability of troops on their left and right to make similar progress. This success was short lived. By the following day their crippled battalions were drifting back into the trenches from which they had leapt forward on a tide of patriotic fervour twenty-four hours earlier. In the time spent here at Thiepval, during the assault and subsequent hours before their units were withdrawn, the 32nd and 36th division suffered more than 9,000 casualties amongst their infantry battalions and associated units. More than 3,000 of those were killed.

South of Thiepval the British faced the twin villages of Ovillers and La Boisselle. Between them these two fortress villages command the approach to the high ground of the Thiepval - Pozières ridge and beyond to Bapaume along the straight Roman road which was initially seen as the focus for the British 'Big Push'. The troops attacking here would have the benefit of a huge width of assaults in either side. The assault on Ovillers would be made by the 8th Division which was confidently expected to be up to the village of Pozières at the end of the morning's fighting.

Ovillers and La Boisselle stood on two shallow spurs of elevated ground which run westwards from the Pozières area. The advantage of that elevation and its command over the broad valleys beneath each spur posed great difficulties here for the attacking British troops. The outcome of that topographical advantage held by the German army was utter devastation to the infantry units in the Mash Valley area. As they advanced down the slopes of the Usna Hill into Mash Valley the soldiers were caught in a maelstrom of direct machine-gun fire from both Ovillers and positions behind La Boisselle.

At La Boisselle, as at Ovillers, there was a huge discrepancy between German casualties and those suffered by British troops attacking towards the

Redan Ridge. *(left)*

This photograph looks across the Auchonvillers to Beaumont Hamel road from the lip of Hawthorn Crater. On the 1 July 1916 the British attacks were made from left to right across No Man's Land which spans the centre of this image. There is no more telling sight on the Somme than a sequence of cemeteries such as this. There is no need to explain. Ever since the 1920s these impeccably maintained cemeteries have stood silent and solemn watch. Unceasingly a steady stream of wives and mothers, fathers, sons, sisters and subsequent generations have come to see just where those men which their villages, collieries, farms and factories had once known had died. This lonely ridge was the scene of the 4th Division's assault on 1 July. More properly it was the location of the objectives of that division's assault. Had that assault been successful the men would have advanced 4,000 metres to Puisieux trench, having crossed the Wagon Road and Munich trench en route. In fact the 4th Division's initial attack succeeded in penetrating the German front lines but their subsequent progress was repulsed and by the end of the day only a tiny fragment of German trench had been captured.

Here on the ridge the German barbed wire glowered menacingly at all who tried to attempt its passage. One man who saw it spoke eloquently of its malevolent qualities.

'The defences of the enemy front line varied a little in degree, but hardly at all in kind, throughout the battlefield. The enemy wire was always deep, thick, and securely staked with iron supports, which were either crossed like the letter X, or upright, with loops to take the wire and shaped at one end like corkscrews so as to screw into the ground. The wire stood on these supports on a thick web, about four feet high and from thirty to forty feet across. The wire used was generally as thick as sailor's marline stuff, or two twisted rope yarns. It contained, as a rule, some sixteen barbs to the foot. The wire used in front of our lines was generally galvanised, and remained grey after months of exposure. The enemy wire, not being galvanised, rusted to a black colour, and shows up black at a great distance. In places this web or barrier was supplemented with trip-wire, or wire placed just above the ground, so that the artillery observing officers might not see it and so not cause it to be destroyed.' [Source. *The Old Front Line*. John Masefield. Spurbooks Ltd. 1919.]

During the succeeding weeks and months the Wagon Road and Munich trench would be fought for on a number of occasions. By November the conditions here were unimaginably severe with glutinous mud making the very act of movement a battle of personal willpower over aching matter.

German lines on 1 July 1916. In military terms the village had been chosen carefully by the German soldiers who came here in 1914. Their trenches ran around the most advantageous positions forming a salient overlooking the two valleys, Mash to its north-west and Sausage to its south. In front of La Boisselle village, on the spur overlooking the two valleys, the trenches were precariously adjacent at the Glory Hole. For months this place had been riven by the detonations of mines and fought across by numerous raiding parties. It was an enormously fearsome and evil place. Careful preparation had been expended by the British to neutralise that dominance astride the Glory Hole by the detonation of mines designed to destroy the most significant German vantage points. The most important were Y Sap, overlooking Mash Valley, and Schwaben Hohe which overlooked Sausage Valley. Under both positions mines had been sunk, the terminal chambers of which were packed with explosives. The detonation of these explosives would precede the assaults by just two minutes. The plan was that, once the 34th Division had fought past the village, the support battalions would leapfrog through on their way to an assault upon the German main Second Position at Contalmaison, two kilometres east of La Boisselle.

In the event the catastrophe which unfolded here meant that La Boisselle became synonymous with wholesale slaughter. During the first few minutes thousands of naive and innocent Kitchener recruits were mown down by machine-gun fire.

South of Sausage Valley the relatively sizable village of Fricourt formed a significant salient for the German army. It was the fulcrum around which the German lines were bent. Above Fricourt the lines ran in a northerly direction towards Serre and Gommecourt. Just south of the village the lines turned to run in an easterly direction. This part of the British battlefront between Fricourt and Montauban was the only area where the British army had comparable observation to the Germans, although the German troops still held the most significant defensive locations along the higher folds and ridges.

The three villages which had become incorporated within the German defensive positions, along the southern arm of the battlefield, were Fricourt, Mametz and Montauban. A little to the south of those complex lines of trenches were the British-held villages of Carnoy and Maricourt. At Maricourt the French army abutted to the right of the British positions. The three divisions which attacked here were the 7th, between Fricourt and Mametz, the 18th, east of Mametz, and the 30th towards Montauban. The 7th and 30th

Beaumont Hamel, Hawthorn Crater, White City and the Sunken Lane. *(opposite)*
This is a series of magnificently interesting locations. The area is full of appeal to visitors and its story is inextricably linked to events at Gallipoli. The reason is simple. By the spring of 1915 the divisions which had seen action on that terrible strip of land were en route for France. Among them was the 29th Division. Serving within that division's battalions were the 1st Lancashire Fusiliers and they would be thrown into action in the valley north of the Hawthorn Crater on the morning of 1 July. There is a very vivid and immensely powerful fictional account of the circumstances in this area in Birdsong *by Sebastian Faulkes.*

Soon after the battle this place was also visited by John Masefield. His evocative descriptions catch something of the sentiments of that post battle weariness and despair.

'This is the crater of the mine of Beaumont Hamel. Until recently it was supposed to be the biggest crater ever blown by one explosion. It is not the deepest: one or two others near La Boisselle are deeper, but none on the Somme field comes near it in bigness and squalor. It is like the crater of a volcano, vast, ragged, and irregular, about one hundred and fifty yards long, one hundred yards across, and twenty-five yards deep. It is crusted and scabbed with yellowish tetter, like sulphur or the rancid fat on meat. The inside has rather the look of meat, for it is reddish and all streaked and scabbed with this pox and with discoloured chalk. A lot of it trickles and oozes like sores discharging pus, and this liquid gathers in holes near the bottom, and is greenish and foul and has the look of dead eyes staring upwards.

... At first sight, on looking into it, it is difficult to believe that it was the work of man; it looks so like nature in her evil mood. It is hard to imagine that only three years ago that hill was corn-field, and the site of the chasm grew bread. After that happy time, the enemy bent his line there and made the salient a stronghold, and dug deep shelters for his men in the walls of his trenches; the marks of the dugouts are still plain in the sides of the pit. Then, on the 1st of July, when the explosion was to be a signal for the attack, and our men waited in the trenches for the spring, the belly of the chalk was heaved, and chalk, clay, dugouts, gear, and enemy, went up in a dome of blackness full of pieces, and spread aloft like a toadstool, and floated, and fell down.' [Source. The Old Front Line. John Masefield. Spurbooks Ltd. 1919.]

Down in the valley, to the north of Hawthorn Crater, is a cemetery whose simple rows of headstones mark many of the Lancashire Fusiliers' casualties. It can be seen clearly from the crater above and it is not hard to imagine how desperately the 29th Division's commanding officer, Major General de Lisle, himself now commanded by Sir Aylmer Hunter Weston who had succeeded to the command of the Corps, wanted success to be ensured by the capture of that prominent position.

The image on the right shows the sunken lane, facing Beaumont Hamel, across which the Lancashire Fusiliers attacked on the morning of 1 July. On the top left horizon trees growing at the site of the Hawthorn Ridge crater can be seen. Geoffrey Malins' position from which he filmed the detonation lay beyond the right of this photograph.

Newfoundland Park. (opposite)
A walk in Newfoundland Park. One of the first things which almost every new visitor to the Somme will do. The park is just a few hundred yards across yet nevertheless it encompasses almost all the history of the 1916 Battles of the Somme. Within its confines are cemeteries containing the graves of men killed on the first day of the campaign and, also, almost its last day.

The 51st Division Memorial. (left) The figure is modelled on that of Company Sergeant Major Bob Rowan, DCM, MBE, C of G (Belgium) of the Gordon Highlanders. He was one of 'The Ladies from Hell'. So went the grudging tribute to the Highlanders from those German units who had faced the determined and ferocious assaults which this division made on numerous occasions during the Great War. The final capture of Beaumont Hamel, on 13 November 1916, was undertaken by the 51st Division's troops. These Highland soldiers were issued with leather aprons to cover their kilts. The unusual dress may initially have amused their opponents, but there was nothing ladylike about the soldiers whose pride in being Scots was enormous. The 51st was a very fine division whose record throughout the war was unremittingly tough, grimly resolved and effective. Unlike the 29th's attempts, four months earlier, the 51st's men were assisted by the deployment of tanks and poison gas which was now freely used by both sides in the conflict.

The Caribou Memorial. (inset opposite) At the start of the Great War Newfoundland was a directly governed province of the British empire. Today Newfoundland is a part of Canada whose flag flies over the park and whose government tends with undiminished care to the maintenance of this park, given in perpetuity by France to commemorate the bravery and sacrifice of so many young Newfoundlanders here on that hot summer's day more than eighty years ago. The Newfoundlanders' sole battalion attacked across the ground now constituting Newfoundland Park. The battalion was composed entirely of native born Newfoundlanders. They had been at Suvla Bay on Gallipoli before being transferred to the 29th Division. During the war years 4,984 men were sent on active service with the battalion. Of those 1,232 were killed, 2,314 wounded and 174 taken prisoner. That is a 75% casualty rate and needs no further comment to reveal the extraordinary sacrifice and willing service of so many people.

Also within the confines of the park are several cemeteries. These are well worth a visit and include Hunter's Cemetery, its tiny plot lies close to the 51st Division's memorial. The comparison between the grandeur of the Highlanders' commemorative statuary and the intimacy of the cemetery is meaningful. Individuals and school parties alike are caught by the simple tragedy of the Black Watch's young soldiers, all killed in front of Beaumont Hamel on 13 November 1916 and tumbled into a waiting shellhole.

divisions contained many Pals units from the great Lancastrian cities of Manchester and Liverpool. At Montauban that combination swept forward in the longest advance made by British troops on 1 July. Unlike the tragedy which enveloped the Ulstermen at the Schwaben Redoubt near Thiepval, the Manchester Pals were able to hold onto their gains. This was the only part of the initial assault which could be defined as a clear success.

One officer caught within the turmoil of events south of Mametz was Lieutenant William Noel Hodgson, bombing officer of the 9th Battalion. William Hodgson was the son of the Right Reverend Henry Hodgson, the first Bishop of Saint Edmundsbury and Ipswich. Lieutenant Hodgson had already been mentioned in despatches before being awarded the Military Cross in October 1915. Hodgson had been educated at Durham School and Christ Church College, Oxford. He was a gifted linguist and poet whose epitaph is also his best known and finest poem, 'Before Action'. For many days the 23-year-old Lieutenant William Hodgson had observed the massive British artillery barrage falling on Mametz, contemplating the moments when the barrage's end would signify the start of the battle. On 29 June, crouched in a filthy dug-out somewhere in the trenches which snaked around Mansell Copse, Hodgson wrote with an unerring poignancy about the forthcoming days and the vivid, terrible contrast with those things that he held dear.

> I, that on my familiar hill
>   Saw with uncomprehending eyes
> A hundred of thy sunsets spill
>   Their fresh and sanguine sacrifice,
> Ere the sun swings his noonday sword
>   Must say good-bye to all of this;-
> By all delights that I shall miss,
>   Help me to die, O Lord

The poem, of which this is the last verse, encapsulates a sense of premonition and inevitability. Most poignantly, in the line 'By all delights that I shall miss', William Hodgson's words gave form to the idea that many men would die without the experience and satisfaction of all that youth should have brought to them. He was killed during the assault on Mametz.

For decades the costs of these events were born by the widows, children, parents and communities of the men who were killed and maimed. The cost to the attackers was immeasurably greater than that to the German defenders at villages like Serre, Thiepval, Ovillers and La Boisselle. The devastating effect of the German's pre-ranged indirect artillery fire, concentrated machine guns with interlocking fields of fire and inappropriate British tactics meant that many men were mown down in No Man's Land before they had time to reach the German trenches.

The assault was broken upon the immensely strong first line of fortifications which had been prepared by the German army. Those professional and hardened soldiers lay in waiting along carefully selected positions making as much use of natural advantage as was possible. Those advantages had been reinforced by months of careful adaptation and digging. Villages from Gommecourt and Serre in the north, past Beaumont Hamel, Thiepval, La Boisselle towards Fricourt and Montauban were incorporated into an immense web of trenches between which the machine guns' complex fields of fire made the movement of troops in the open and daylight fraught with terrible danger. Tragically little trust was placed in the British soldier's initiative and combat skill by his senior commanders - the tactics were barren of innovation.

The statistics generated by that day are immense. On the British side

Thiepval and the Ulster Tower. *(opposite)*
German troops within the village of Thiepval held firm throughout the first days of battle. Subsequently this high ground became the new fulcrum around which the focus of British endeavours swung during the late July and August battles. It was not until late September that the village and the baleful Schwaben Redoubt were finally captured. After the war the Ulster Tower was built to commemorate the brave but ultimately unsuccessful assault of the Ulster men north of Thiepval.

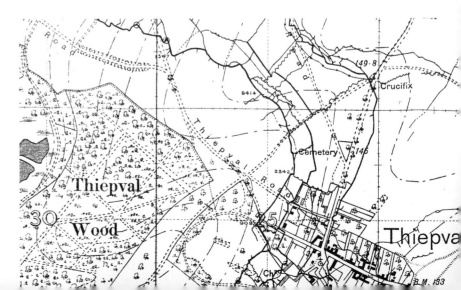

almost 60,000 casualties. Amongst these more than 20,000 had been killed or posted as missing[4]. It was the bleakest day in British military history, and certainly the bleakest day in Britain's 20th century social history as well.

There is one extraordinary fact about the positions below Serre village, at the northern end of the battlefield, that it is ultimately essential to dwell upon a while. It deals with the futility and unpredictability of war. These places had been the starting point for some of the most northerly attacks on the 1916 Somme battlefield. And yet, for all the ferocity of that fighting and the intensity of combat which subsequently unfolded within the woods and valleys to the south, nothing moved at Railway Hollow beneath Serre. It was only the following spring, after a harrowing and immensely cold winter, that the German army pulled back from the Somme battlefield. Behind they left a trail of devastation across which the British and French armies were forced to advance before coming up against a newly prepared line of defences, the Hindenburg Line. During the spring of 1917 the British Army fought another massive engagement whose purpose was to outflank those lines. That was the Battle of Arras. The battle for Passchendaele east of Ypres was still to come.

Soon after the events of 1 July the approaches to the southern aspect of the battlefield became the busiest part of the contested zone, filling with the materiel and logistics of war – supplies – the very lifeblood of an army. The terrible scale of the casualties incurred on 1st July were not allowed to deflect the imperative for offensive action. Maintaining momentum was essential to the prospects for military success. Never in the history of human conflict had such vast quantities of materiel been assembled to support the diverse processes of warfare and the appalling business of the soldiers who did it. None of what the infantry did would have been possible without the Quartermasters. At its simplest the Quartermaster's task was to feed the men. Each battalion had a Field Kitchen and transports to service the men's elemental needs. When in the lines their food was invariably cold and greasy and all too often soiled by the summer chalk dust which was the inevitable concomitant of conflict here on the Somme.

✦ ✦ ✦

Ovillers and La Boisselle. (opposite)

The two villages of Ovillers and La Boisselle are inseparable. They gaze at each other in perpetuity across what British soldiers once knew as Mash Valley. On the far side of La Boisselle, en route for Fricourt, you will find the inevitable and corresponding Sausage Valley!

Although the slaughter here on the morning of 1 July garnered a ghastly proportion of the British participants there are relatively few cemeteries here to mark the inhumane suffering of the many thousands who fell in these fields. The most visible is Ovillers Military Cemetery which today lies in what was No Man's Land in front of Ovillers village. The troops attacking across this place on 1 July were the 2nd Devons. To their south the 2nd Middlesex were devastated in Mash Valley; their commanding officer would later commit suicide whilst in London, utterly depressed about the predictable tragedy he had witnessed here. It took two further weeks of the most intense and violent fighting, and the engagement of five British divisions, before Ovillers finally fell on the night of 15/16 July.

In the coming weeks, after the fighting had moved eastwards, officers walking this area found whole sections of men, still in their parade ground straight lines, rigid and still where they had fallen. In their assault against less than two miles of front line the 8th and 34th Divisions lost thousands of men on 1 July. Figures published in the Official History make clear what a terrible event had occurred: 11,501 casualties in total; more than 4,000 men killed. The city of Newcastle-upon-Tyne paid a terrible price. The initial assault upon La Boisselle was made by the Tyneside Scottish Brigade. The subsequent advance towards Contalmaison was to be made by the Tyneside Irish Brigade. Very few men of either brigade, some eight battalions, got beyond the German wire. A sizable proportion of the Tyneside Irish were hit before they even approached the British front line trenches.

After the war the process of battlefield clearance resulted in the creation of large and somewhat impersonal cemeteries in this area. Into those cemeteries the tiny clusters of graves scattered around almost every fold in the ground were concentrated into cemeteries like Ovillers Military and 'Gordon Dump' Cemetery. Such colloquial names often hark back to a location well known to the troops, usually a prominence or a strong point named on one of the many thousands of trench maps created to make sense of this battle-torn landscape. At Ovillers Military Cemetery the graves are principally of British troops, although the low walls also contain many French graves, those of men killed in the area during 1914/15 before the British army arrived to take over this previously quiet sector.

---

4. The official history reports 19,240 killed, 35,493 wounded, 2,152 missing and 585 prisoners of war. 57,470 casualties in total.

during the summer and autumn of 1916, to marshal so many soldiers into one collective act of willpower. There soon began a series of major engagements, many of which were massive set-piece battles in their own right, which collectively became the Battles of the Somme. Whilst the principal axis on 1 July had been along the Bapaume road, it had now became apparent that limited successes along the southern arm of the battlefield that day, from Fricourt - Mametz towards Montauban and beyond into the French sector, had to be exploited. In the early stages of the Battles of the Somme, as the fighting progressed north of Carnoy and Montauban towards Mametz Wood and the Longueval Ridge, the Carnoy valley, along the road between Albert and Péronne, became home to dozens of supply units. The whole area burgeoned with Nissen huts and vast encampments of tents to house whole brigades of men, huge dumps of artillery shells, salvaged equipment, mountains of petrol canisters filled with foul and stagnant water for the fighting troops, boxes containing millions of Small Arms Ammunition rounds, grenades, trench mortar bombs, medical stores and component spares for vehicles, guns and personal equipment. From out of Dernancourt, in the Ancre valley, railway lines crept forward, with each advance of the fighting front, past Morlancourt and up to the Carnoy - Mametz area.

Fighting men and their supplies were pressed forward into the pitched battles for control of what one eminent historian often calls the 'Great Horseshoe of Woods'. Throughout the remainder of July these woods were fought for with malevolent ferocity as the British Army sought to wrest command of the high ground and its priceless artillery observation and control from German hands. This next phase was therefore a battle for the German Army's Second Positions even though many of the first line positions had not fallen in the first phase of the battle.

The initial woods to be fought for included Bernafay and Trones, later the grim Mametz Wood, making way for the huge dawn attack on Longueval and the Bazentin Ridge on the morning of 14 July. That day British cavalry entered High Wood but were repulsed by German troops desperate to maintain their hold upon this central and superb vantage point.

The innovative and brilliantly executed assault of 14 July marks the end of what many regard as the first phase of the Battle of the Somme. Now it was the turn of Delville Wood, which had stood beyond the right flank of the attack on 14 July, and High Wood, in its central position of dominance on the 1916 battlefield a little to the north-west of Delville Wood. In both these locations, which became grim synonyms for the word carnage, a terrible concentration of close combat and killing went on for days upon seemingly endless days. Delville Wood became the scene for a genuinely heroic struggle undertaken for control of that wood involving South African troops. It would be weeks before these positions were cleared of German troops. Those men's resilience, indomitable bravery and determination to hold on at all costs were almost beyond comprehension.

Fricourt and Mametz. (opposite)

South of Mametz is one of the smallest and yet most frequently visited cemeteries on the Somme battlefield. This is the Devonshires' cemetery at Mansell Copse. It is nothing more than a battlefield burial of men killed in the attempt to storm Mametz. The brutality and simplicity of the circumstances always move the emotions of the cemetery's many visitors. On 1 July 1916 the Devons were due to move in a north-westerly direction past the southern end of Mametz village. The bulk of the Devons' men were killed by machine-gun fire emanating from the village's communal cemetery where a shrine had been put to use as both disguise and protection for machine gunners beneath. Nearby is another small battlefield burial, that of the 2nd Gordon Highlanders. At the end of the war there were many more such proud but isolated burials, where small groups of perhaps twenty or thirty comrades were interred together. However, apart from these two small cemeteries south of Mametz, the rest were removed, the bodies exhumed, to be concentrated into Danzig Alley cemetery east of Mametz.

Entry is gained along a well-trodden and rather worn pathway which leads up an embankment. Once there, you are looking along the site of the 9th Devon's front line trench. At the far end you will find the grave of Captain Duncan Martin who led A Company into their attack that fateful morning. Following the attack by the 9th Devons, and that of the 8th Battalion in support, the survivors buried the regiment's dead here in the front line trench. That service took place on 4 July. Ten of the Devon's men were unidentifiable. The cemetery contains one officer of the 8th Battalion who had been killed on 28 June, along with three officers and 34 other ranks who were killed on 1 July. The 9th Battalion's casualties on 1 July included six officers and 116 other ranks who are buried here, together with one officer of the 11th Battalion, 2nd Lieutenant William Riddle, who was also killed here that day. The cemetery also contains the graves of two men killed later in the Somme battles, whilst serving with B Battery, 92 Brigade RFA. The poet, Noel Hodgson is also amongst those buried here. After Hodgson's death a posthumous volume of his work was published under the title 'Verse and Prose in Peace and War'.

The photograph of Mansel Copse shows the valley which Lieutenant Hodgson overlooked from his positions in and above the small wooded copse. Whilst the war overwhelmed Hodgson and so many of his contemporaries, the landscape here has survived and today provides a wonderful and elevating passage amidst incredible and thought-provoking history. That survival is part of the Somme's enduring appeal. Tracing the simplicity of human events is to understand a signal event in man's recent history. This is where so many of our roots lie. From India, New Zealand, Australia, Canada and Britain a whole generation passed through this place. It is not hard to sense those men's presence when you stand here.

CHAPTER FOUR

SOMME 2

Friends are good on the Day of Battle

At the start of the Battles of the Somme the town of Albert lay just behind the British front line positions and west of the epicentre of the British effort directed towards Pozières. Railway facilities ended at the nearby village of Dernancourt where the huge logistical initiative to support the British front line troops was centred. That village lay within the once picturesque and tranquil Ancre valley. Further to the west lay other little-known hamlets, Buire, Heilly and the more important town of Corbie, all with dozens of medical facilities, operating theatres, casualty clearing stations and the terrible logical corollaries – the cemeteries. Throughout the months of battle those places listened to the hiss of the locomotives, idling time as a steady stream of casualties were carried within. From their windows dozens of dedicated nurses caught glimpses of tired dust-laden battalions marching to and from the cauldron of battle.

Those who had time to look up from their work south-west of Albert in the Ancre valley could see the flickering hues of orange and blue as the gunner's shells danced upon the horizons to the east. The high ground of the Pozières ridge, the dominating heights of Thiepval's broad shoulders, the smoking blackness of splintered woodlands. All were played upon by the terrible shards of steel which vented from every clanging, crashing, tortured explosion. At night the stars were more than matched by the glare of Very lights, SOS rockets and parachute flares whose varied luminescence gave colour to the deadly games of patrols in No Man's Land under the deep monochrome of night. Those whose nerves would allow slept by day. Men's faces took on the gaunt expressions of despair and loss.

Every day of the Somme campaign was marked by attempts, somewhere on the battlefield, to advance. The spirit of offensive action was deemed paramount by the British and French commands during the 1916 Somme campaign. 'No respite' for the German defences - but no respite for Tommy either! That is not to say, however, that the efforts of the British High Command were marked by a lurid and pointless willingness to sacrifice huge numbers of men in the aimless pursuit of attritional success. Only by looking carefully at the battlefield and seeing the immense tactical difficulties faced by all who sought to advance across terrain networked and crossed with an immense complexity of trenches, shell-proof shelters, machine-gun posts, barbed wire, sunken lanes hiding dug-outs full of determined men and the ever present artillery in support can you begin to take in the enormity of these battles.

Within and dominating the open acres of battlefield were the woodlands. It would be difficult for us to visualise them some eighty years ago, riven by great shards of steel which had torn branches away and left huge trunks splintered into stiletto sharp daggers of hardwood. The leaves were withered by gas and cordite whose chemical smells combined evilly with the stench of corruption. Buried within were trench lines invisible to the eyes of haggard

Crucifix Corner (opposite)
Situated near the farm of Bazentin le Grand, this was a vital junction for troops going up the line to attack High Wood and Longueval. The Christ figure is pitted with marks left by shrapnel and bullets.

men who sought to fight their way through. Concrete had been used to reinforce the command bunkers and machine-gun posts which glowered defiantly within the wood's wreckage. And in the height of summer the clouds of flies could be heard buzzing excitedly at the unexpected torrent of corpses which they fed upon and laid their eggs within. The first such wood to become the focus of intense fighting was Mametz Wood.

Whilst the village of Mametz had fallen on 1st July, the capture of the wood behind the village posed enormous tactical difficulties for the British Army. Since the focus of the British effort was now determined by the relative success of their attacks along the southern arm of the battlefield, on 1 July, the great weight of subsequent attacks was thrown northwards into that critical horseshoe of woods which surrounded the Bazentin villages. The three most southerly of those woods were Mametz and, further east past Montauban, Bernafay Wood and Trones Wood. The capture of these became an imperative precursor to the planned dawn assault on 14 July, between the Bazentin villages and Longueval, which would signal the start of the second phase of the Somme battles. However, within each wood's confines the advantage to the defence would be enormous. And significantly, the approach to Mametz Wood lay over open ground within the valley of the Willow Stream. Its languid sounding name belied the terror which troops finding themselves within its confines would experience in the period between 5 and 11 July 1916. That was the week in which Lloyd George's Welsh Army, the 38th Division, came of age.

Initially the attacks on the approaches to the wood were made by units which had spearheaded the opening of the campaign south of Mametz Wood. To the south-east that was the 18th Division, whilst south of the wood it was the 7th Division. The first part of the assaults upon the wood focused on the need to get past its western side towards Contalmaison and the 17th Division suffered terrible casualties during these events, the presence of enfilade fire from German troops in Mametz Wood invariably making such attacks costly. On 5 July one incident was destined to become well known. It involved a Second Lieutenant serving with the 1st Royal Welsh Fusiliers. This battalion was a regular unit - not part of 38th Division whose soldiers were, by comparison, 'half trained civilians'. The 1st Royal Welsh Fusiliers were working with the 2nd Royal Irish to occupy Wood Trench by bombing along to the left in Quadrangle Trench towards Wood Trench.

'There wasn't much wire in front of Quadrangle Trench. I entered
it at a strongpoint on the extreme left and exploring to the right I

Triangle Point to High Wood. (opposite)

There are many locations where you can sense the tides of history. This is one such. To the casual visitor Triangle Point is little more than an unfamiliar corner of a quietly agrarian community. But to the Kitchener men who were the backbone of the British Army in 1916 Triangle Point marks the summit of their determination, bravery and success on 1 July. It is an appropriate place to start our journey into the subsequent events of the Battles of the Somme.

The attacks upon the nearby village of Montauban were undertaken by the 30th Division. On their right were the French Army. The 30th Division was comprised mainly of Pals units from the industrial and commercial heartlands of Manchester and Liverpool. Rawlinson, Fourth Army's commanding officer, was not optimistic about this New Army division's chances, yet when their assault was made the men carried all their objectives in a magnificent feat of arms. Advancing further than any other unit on 1 July, the Manchester Pals secured the Triangle Point positions. From here they could see all of the great horseshoe of woods spread in front, across the Longueval Ridge and beyond.

Those woods and the high ground of the Pozières Ridge would become the cauldron at the heart of the 1916 battlefield.

But, frustratingly, this advantageous situation could not be capitalised upon. Rawlinson was unprepared for success here and no immediate pressure was applied to the shattered German lines in the area of the Bazentin villages or across the Longueval Ridge. Costly attacks now became necessary on the horseshoe's outlying woods, Mametz, Bernafay and Trones, as preliminaries to the enormous and successful Dawn Attack, on 14th July, on the Bazentin Ridge. That day British troops reached High Wood but were unable to hold their exposed positions. Thereafter thousands of British troops moved through Triangle Point on their way 'Up the Line' to join the intense and unwavering conflicts which raged in and around the vicinity of High Wood.

On the horizon is Caterpillar Valley Cemetery. It is both imposing and fascinating. The cemetery lies close to Longueval village on the low ridge overlooking Caterpillar Valley. When the Manchester Pals captured Montauban on 1 July they looked north across that valley, from Triangle Point, to see German troops fleeing into the sanctuary of Longueval and the trenches astride the ridge where the cemetery stands today.

This enormous burial ground results from the fighting during both 1916 and 1918. Whilst most British cemeteries here date from 1916, Caterpillar Valley is very different. Its purpose spans the entire range of commemorative and memorial intent. Within its walls are an original cluster of 38th Division graves, dug during the August of 1918 as the British army forced the German forces from these ridges for the last time in the Great War. It also houses the poignant New Zealand memorial to the missing of September and October 1918. Many of these men had been at Gallipoli in 1915. By the time of their death, just weeks before the war's end, they had been overseas away from their farms and villages on the far side of the planet for four desolate years. However, the bulk of the graves, concentrated here after the war, date from 1916.

found young Fernby.

Kendle, who had been trying to do something for a badly wounded man, now rejoined me, and we continued, mostly on all fours, along the dwindling trench. The trench became a shallow groove and ended where the ground overlooked a little valley along which there was a light railway line. We stared across at the Wood. From the other side of the valley came an occasional rifle-shot, and a helmet bobbed up for a moment. The helmet bobbed up again. "I'll just have a shot at him," he said wriggling away from the crumbling bank which gave us cover. At this moment Fernby appeared with two men and a Lewis gun. Kendle was half kneeling against some broken ground; I remember seeing him push his tin hat back from his forehead and then raise himself a few inches to take aim. After firing

The innocence of this photograph belies the great effort and risk involved in capturing such a fortified machine gun postion. This one, heavily capped with concrete, was located close to Mametz Wood.

once he looked at us with a lively smile; a second later he fell sideways. A blotchy mark showed where the bullet had hit him just above the eyes.

The circumstances being what they were, I had no justification for feeling either shocked or astonished by the sudden extinction of Lance-Corporal Kendle. But after blank awareness that he was killed, all feelings tightened and contracted to a single intention - "to settle that sniper" on the other side of the valley. If I had stopped to think, I shouldn't have gone at all. As it was, I discarded my tin hat and equipment, slung a bag of bombs across my shoulder, abruptly informed Fernby that I was going to find out who was there, and set off at a downhill double. While I was running I pulled the safety-pin out of a Mills bomb; my right hand being loaded, I did the same for my left. I mention this because I was obliged to extract the second safety-pin with my teeth, and the grating sensation reminded me that I was halfway across and not so reckless as I had been when I started. I was even a little out of breath as I trotted up the opposite slope. Just before I arrived at the top I slowed up and threw my two bombs. Then I rushed at the bank, vaguely expecting some sort of scuffle with my imagined enemy. I had lost my temper with the man who had shot Kendle; quite unexpectedly, I found myself looking down into a well-conducted trench with a great many Germans in it. Fortunately for me, they were already retreating. It had not occurred to them that they were being attacked by a single fool; and Fernby, with presence

Mametz Wood. *(opposite)*

Between the 5th and 11th July the Welshmen endured a terrifying ordeal within the confines of Mametz Wood. Although other divisions were occupied in part with this fighting it was Lloyd George's Welsh Army, the 38th Division, whose gallantry and sacrifice are enduringly associated with this place. Close nearby, to the east of Mametz Wood, stands Flat Iron Copse. Here there is a substantial cemetery made especially poignant by the burial within of three sets of brothers, Tregaskis, Hardwidge and Philby.

On the south of the wood lies the Welsh Dragon memorial. Bathed in misted morning light or the golden glow of a clear evening this is one of the most vivid memorials standing upon the British sector of the Somme battlefield. The need for such a memorial was almost overlooked and its existence today is a reminder of just how enduring is the need to understand and record the events of 1916 and their part in Britain's social and military history. During a visit to the battlefield one veteran of the fighting, Sergeant Tom Price, was stunned to find that no memorial to his fellow soldiers' exploits existed. This was made good by the efforts of many Welsh people. The proud and defiant work of sculptor David Peterson now looks out across the Hammerhead and Death Valley.

of mind which probably saved me, had covered my advance by traversing the top of the trench with his Lewis gun. I slung a few more bombs, but they fell short of the clumsy field-grey figures, some of whom had turned to fire their rifles over the left shoulder as they ran across the open toward the wood, while a crowd of jostling helmets vanished along the trench.

Having thus failed to commit suicide, I proceeded to occupy the trench - that is to say, I sat down on the fire-step, very much out of breath, and hoped to God the Germans wouldn't come back again.'

The Second Lieutenant who recounted this story was Siegfried Sassoon. When he finally returned to Bottom Wood he incurred the ill temper of his battalion commanding officer who pointed out that Sassoon's presence in the enemy trench had held up an artillery bombardment for three hours! However, his bravery was never doubted by the men and officers with whom he served; yet Sassoon's critical and sensitive mind was quite capable of seeing the futility of the war which now enveloped him. And it was the imminent arrival of the Welsh citizen army which would prompt Sassoon's antagonism to the ways in which war fouled that citizenry's humanity. Sassoon's subsequent opposition to the war's continuance made him the object of much ill will, both public and governmental.

When the 38th Division were brought into events here at Mametz Wood, relieving the exhausted 7th Division's men, they weren't thought of as much by those experienced hands. Again Sassoon's incisive words capture the feelings of the moment:

'They were mostly undersized men and as I watched them

High Wood. (below and opposite)
Nowhere on the 1916 Somme battlefield did the vehement nature of the fighting leave behind a more sinister aspect than here. The location is not quite the most elevated position on the battlefield, the one higher being just east of Pozières at the windmill on the crest of the Thiepval - Pozières ridge. High Wood is inaccessible to visitors, perhaps no bad thing in that within are still the remains of many thousands of unrecovered bodies. In a sequence of plaintive gestures, revealing the loss and pride of numerous units which came here, there are a sequence of memorials in the area commemorating the participation of British soldiers from as far afield as London and the highlands of Scotland.

The written histories of this place are scattered with the sentiment of missed opportunity. Following the capture of the Longueval Ridge on 14 July this place could and should have been taken into British control. That day saw the only significant deployment of cavalry during 1916, but the 7th Dragoon Guards and Deccan Horse were quickly cut down and stopped by machine-gun fire. The infantry which did enter the wood were driven out that night. The next two months were a period of unremitting anguish for the Tommies who came here. Like the worst locations in the Ypres Salient it seemed to men allotted the unenviable task of advancing towards this malevolent and menacing place that their death warrant had been signed. The final capture of the wood was undertaken by the 47th (London) Division during an enormous attack on 15 September.

If those who come here need any testimony to the severity of the fighting it should suffice to know that after the Second World War, an event which added 146 additional soldiers and airmen to the total within the nearby London cemetery, a further 890 Great War bodies were discovered in this vicinity. Of the 3,769 Great War soldiers buried here 3,112 are unidentified.

(Opposite) The tangle of unkempt saplings and trunks within High Wood - The Bois des Fourcaux - Raven's Wood. Still hidden within is the wreckage of a German machine-gun position.

arriving at the first stage of their battle experience I had a sense of their victimisation. A little platoon officer was settling his men down with a valiant show of self-assurance. For the sake of appearances orders of some kind had to be given, though in reality there was nothing to do except sit down and hope it wouldn't rain. He spoke sharply to some of them, and I felt that they were like a lot of children. It was going to be a bad look-out for two such bewildered companies, huddled up in the Quadrangle, which had been over-garrisoned by our own comparatively small contingent. Visualising that forlorn crowd of khaki figures under the twilight of the trees, I can believe that I saw then, for the first time, how blindly war destroys its victims. The sun had gone down on my own reckless brandishings, and I understood the doomed condition of these half trained civilians who had been sent up to attack the Wood.'

In great part it was the sacrifice of thousands of Welsh lives which paved the

Delville Wood - the Bois d'Elville. *(above and opposite)*

When I first saw Ed Skelding's photograph of a mist rolling across the fields adjacent to Delville Wood it seemed a perfect synopsis of the Somme's timeless enchantment. I never tire of the woodlands here, especially in the early mornings of autumn when their colours change from pastel shades to the vivid and redolent hues of autumn. Within yards of this place there is a busy and much visited centre whose facilities draw throngs of people throughout the year. People seeking solace and reflection are catered for just as well. The woods are crossed by a sequence of wide paths or rides within which you can stroll for hours, with little chance of meeting another person. It is, quite simply, a very beautiful and lovely woodland scene. You might, perchance, meet the old hornbeam whose knowing face has seen it all, the only tree to survive the carnage amongst its fellows and the soldiers who fought it out amongst them.

Yet it was not always thus. After Longueval Ridge's capture during great Dawn Attack of 14 July this wood became the scene of an immensely difficult and personal struggle at close quarters until its final capture on 28 July. Four divisions came here to take part in these grim events, but it was the South Africans, as part of the 9th Scottish Division, whose exploits have lingered most enduringly. They came here with 121 officers and 3,032 other ranks. They left with 29 officers and 751 men.

way for the successful assault upon the Bazentin Ridge at dawn on 14 July.

Subsequently, from 15 July, fighting within Delville Wood marked a new nadir in man's inhumanity. The stench of decomposition and the appalling sights of death and destruction were born with stoicism by men suddenly forced to contemplate events utterly beyond their peacetime experience. It was not unusual for battalions thrown in 800 riflemen strong to suffer more than 500 casualties - sometimes even worse. The conflict took on the mantle of attrition. Of course it would be too simple to say that success would be measured solely on the weighing scales of death, but the idea that the war, or even just this battle, would be won solely by the progressive occupation of another few thousand yards of trench was palpably out of touch if not nonsensical. What had begun in an atmosphere of great optimism was slipping inexorably into a self-perpetuating contest, where victory was measured as much by not losing as by any other criteria.

After two weeks of fighting Delville Wood was secured. Already, by 23 July, the second phase of the battle was engaged. Pozières, Longueval and Guillemont were the objectives of enormous British military effort. By 26th July Pozières village, close to the highest point of the Albert to Bapaume road and a crucial part of the German Second Position, was in British hands. Initially it had been hoped, imagined, that this village would be captured before 10.00 am on 1st July!

. By August 1916 the fighting on the British part of the Somme battlefield centred around villages which lay on the still-uncaptured German main Second Positions such as Guillemont and Ginchy. The terrible exchanges of

By the autumn of 1916 artillery shells had reduced the once splendid trees of Delville Wood to jagged shards and lifeless splinters.

artillery and the seemingly unremitting intensity of front line duty and infantry assault made this period one of almost unendurable nightmare for the Tommy and his counterparts in the French and German armies.

Throughout those two months of fighting, during which repeated attempts were made by soldiers of numerous divisions to capture Guillemont, British trenches were slowly advanced closer and closer to the outlying fringes of the village. In a terrible travesty of humanity the perpetual shelling made it almost impossible to evacuate wounded men from this area in daylight. Whilst it is impossible to mention anything other than an infinitesimal fragment of the human suffering experienced here I do want to give proper credit to one battalion's part in these events. They were the 2nd Royal Scots Fusiliers, a lowland regiment who wore the standard khaki service trousers and puttees which distinguished them from their highland counterparts.   As part of the 30th Division they had already taken a conspicuous part in the fighting for Montauban and Trones Wood. When that division was thrust forward into Guillemont on 30 July it was the 2nd Royal Scots Fusiliers who led the way. Catastrophically for those brave and hard-fighting men, it proved quite impossible for other nearby units to maintain positions on the Royal Scots Fusiliers' flanks. The Official History describes what happened as the day lengthened:

'In spite of the barrages laid by the heavy artillery on the cross-roads east of the village and round Leuze Wood and Ginchy, the Germans were now coming forward to counter-attack; but it was difficult for the British batteries to fire on Guillemont, where three companies of the Royal Scots Fusiliers still held out. Unfortunately the reserves of both brigades had been expended and defensive considerations were now paramount; so the Fusiliers, cut off by the German defensive barrage and deprived of all support and assistance, were eventually overwhelmed. This battalion, which had pressed on with such splendid resolution to its objective, deserved a better fate. There is ample evidence that it was not easily overcome.'

The battalion paid a dear price for its success. Two hundred officers and men were killed and many men taken into captivity. Of the 200 killed only 11 have known burial places, the remainder being commemorated on the Thiepval Memorial.

Throughout the battles for Guillemont individual examples of genuine heroism abound. Captain Noel Chavasse, V.C., and bar, M.C., was the 1/10th King's inspirational medical officer. He was the son of the Bishop of Liverpool and, before the war, an outstanding athlete at Oxford. In the forlorn ground

Mouquet Farm. (left and opposite)
Mucky Farm. Behind Thiepval on the German main Second Position. The Salford Pals' objective on day one of the Somme offensive. Finally secured on 26 September 1916, almost three months into that drawn-out affair with death. But August was the month during which the farm saw the most savage fighting after the very highest ground on the Albert - Bapaume road, north-east of Pozières had been captured by the Australians on 5 August. These were the same men who had been so adroitly evacuated from Gallipoli and who were now experiencing their baptism of fire on the Western Front. Throughout those hot days it was the ANZACs who then repeatedly threw themselves into the grotesque stinking sea of churned soil, subterranean passages and shell-shattered cellars which made up the Mouquet Farm sector.

The Official Historian granted these resilient men a few words of praise, perhaps subconsciously ascribing some of those personal characteristics which had shown through so vividly in the heat of Gallipoli.

'...Australia has every reason to be proud of the devotion and gallantry of her troops in the fiery ordeal of the Somme battle...the men had proved themselves skilful and self-reliant - if at times over-reckless fighters...' [Military Operations. France and Belgium. 1916. Vol II.]

The significance of the Mouquet Farm positions was never lost upon their German defenders. Its defence was a matter of principle and military necessity. Once Mouquet Farm was lost it would only be a matter of time before the Schwaben Redoubt, north of Thiepval, fell.

between Trônes Wood and Guillemont Noel Chavasse would win the first of his two Victoria Crosses. No man was more valorous and brave than this extraordinary human being. Within the context of the Great War's almost unimaginable squalor he gave everything in an unstinting devotion to the process of saving life. The citation for his award gives only the most distant flavour of the strength, purpose and resolve Noel Chavasse deployed here at Guillemont. An action undertaken on the night of 8/9 August was the scene. During the day he watched three of the battalion's doomed charges. That evening Captain Noel Chavasse took a group of his stretcher-bearers out into No Man's Land in front of Guillemont and began the process of trying to identify the dead and succour the wounded. Throughout the night Chavasse's team worked on, inspired by his cool good-natured manner. As he searched the shattered terrain Chavasse brought his characteristic qualities of

A British soldier lies crumpled in death at Guillemont. Photographers were discouraged from picturing severe wounds. This soldier's only visible damage appears to be his right wrist.

humanity and dedication to the gruesome task in hand. Eventually dawn forced abandonment and Chavasse returned. The subsequent citation, published in the *London Gazette* on 26 October 1916, spoke of the dignified and determined valour which Noel Chavasse had shown whilst carrying out his duties.

'During an attack he tended the wounded in the open all day, under heavy fire, frequently in view of the enemy. During the ensuing night he searched for wounded on the ground in front of the enemy's lines for four hours. Next day he took one stretcher-bearer to the advanced trenches, and, under heavy fire, carried an urgent case for 500 yards into safety, being wounded in the side by a shell splinter during the journey. The same night he took up a party of trusty volunteers, rescued three wounded men from a shell-hole twenty-five yards from the enemy's trench, buried the bodies of two officers, and collected many identity discs, although fired on by bombs and machine guns. Altogether he saved the lives of some twenty badly wounded men, besides the ordinary cases which passed through his hands. His courage and self-sacrifice were beyond praise.'

On a similar personal and singular scale I want to note a very different sort of event. The scene was during the late afternoon of 12 August, amidst fine hot weather, when the 55th Division attempted another attack on the Maltz Horn knoll south of Guillemont. The objective was to secure the higher ground on the Hardecourt road in order to ensure that further frontal attacks on the village were not exposed to enfilade fire from their right. On the left flank of the British lines facing these positions the trenches were being held by the 1/7th King's men who heard the divisional artillery begin its bombardment at 3.30 pm. Almost immediately the German artillery fire increased in intensity. Nevertheless, the attack was made successfully at 5.15 pm under the

The view to Ginchy from Guillemont. *(opposite)*
If High Wood has the distinction, if that can possibly be the correct word, of being the most inhospitable and evil woodland which was fought for during the Somme campaign, then Guillemont is probably the holder of a similar distinction as the most notorious village within the German main Second Positions. Unlike High Wood, Guillemont village does not occupy a position of dominating higher ground, but its complex natural folds made the area ideally sited for defence, and the approaches from the direction of Trônes Wood were at all times dominated by ever-watchful German artillery units.

Today it is a few casual moments' stroll from the eastern border of Trônes Wood, captured by the night of 13/14 July, to the western extremities of the village. Yet it was not until 3 September, eight weeks later, that Guillemont was finally made secure.

protection of an intense bombardment. Unfortunately the expected French advance at Maurepas and the ravine failed to materialise and the 1/9th King's men who made the advance were eventually forced to withdraw since their right flank was utterly exposed. Late on 13 August the King's soldiers in this vicinity were relieved.

Earlier that same day, at 10.00 am, the young Second Lieutenant Jack Fearnhead was hit, possibly by two bullets, one of which penetrated his lung. The trenches were so shallow from the devastating effects of shelling that it proved impossible for him to be removed during daylight hours. The stretcher-bearers of the 5th South Lancs dressed Jack's wounds while he was conscious, probably believing it to be superficial, and promised to return that night to evacuate him. The likelihood is that the 5th South Lancs men were very hard-pressed that day and Jack Fearnhead slipped into unconsciousness unnoticed. On the stretcher-bearers' return he was found to be dead. Like so many other young men who were killed here at Guillemont his grave is unmarked. Jack's company commander, Captain R.G.Thompson, said in his letter of condolence that 'They buried him on the spot, and collected his identity disc and personal belongings... I am afraid that it is not likely that the burial party will have been able to mark the grave, but it was at a spot a bare half mile south of Guillemont.'

By now the vestiges of optimism had withered. Incredibly, above the banks of the River Ancre, the German fortress which was Thiepval village was still unvisited by British troops. Its positions overlooked all that the British army coveted. Thiepval's capture would, of necessity, have to be undertaken. Above all the weather had not, as yet, played anything more than a random hand in events.

In terms of the casualties suffered both sides had indeed suffered badly. By the end of August the British Adjutant General reported that 196,277 officers and men had become casualties. The French had suffered more than 70,000, the Germans, according to British Intelligence returns, more than 200,000.

By 3 September Guillemont was, after repeated attempts, finally captured. This was a day when severe fighting for control of High Wood was still

Flers. (opposite)

On that epic highway which runs eastwards from Albert a steady rumble of vehicles pass the villages of Ovillers, La Boisselle, Pozières, Courcelette and le Sars before reaching the Butte de Warlencourt. In just eleven kilometres, a few short minutes' drive, this encompasses the story of the Battle of the Somme. Many visitors find it exasperating that such a trivial distance in today's increasingly accessible and small world could have exercised a generation of young men in such an unenviable and costly battle of attrition. This seamless and rolling topography mark the place as simply unremarkable. It is the inconsequentiality of this landscape which appears at first glance to sit so uneasily with the momentous nature of the battle fought out across this terrain.

A short distance south-east of the Butte de Warlencourt is one somnolent and archetypal example of a Somme village. This is Flers. Its communal cemetery and timeless busyness with matters agricultural tell that no matter what events have wrought havoc here during the 20th century's most influential war, the central matters in man's existence are, and always will be, the feeding of our children and the rearing of the next generation of young people. Flers' people go about their daily matters indifferent to the interest of passers by. Yet in the late stages of the 1916 battle this village saw an event almost as significant as the first use of gas in Ypres during 1915. This was the scene of the first successful deployment of tanks in numbers. It was on 15 September 1916.

The battle for Flers was begun only after the fall of the two woods which protected its western approaches, Delville and High woods. The open nature of the ground, the relatively fine weather and the use of a fresh infantry division, the 41st, were essential elements in this story because the tanks had already acquired notoriety from their unreliable and temperamental manners. When used singly in previous attacks they had become easy prey to the German gunners. The tanks' crews were exceptionally brave men who operated these primitive beasts in a choking and overheated atmosphere of cordite, petrol and exhaust fumes. Here at Flers that bravery brought success and showed the way forward to succeeding wars as infantry followed in the wake of an armoured advance.

The tanks belonged to D Company of the Heavy Branch Machine Gun Corps. Thirteen started out from near to the Bois d'Elville. Progressively they were whittled away by breakdowns, shellfire and becoming ditched across cavernous trenches, but six ground their way into Flers village, and three almost to Gueudecourt. The infantry was galvanised and immensely enthused by the lumbering giants' success. The village's main street, indeed its only street, witnessed scenes of wild enthusiasm as the inexperienced 41st Division's men, in their first real attack, cheered the tanks on.

It was an event quite without precedent, revealing in an instant the potency of this new weapon of war.

continuing! Two days later the last parts of the German Army's Second Position in that area were in British hands. By 15th September the Third Phase of the Somme battle was initiated and tanks were deployed for the first time. High Wood was finally secured, the villages of Flers, Courcelette and Martinpuich were taken. North of the Bapaume road the fortress of Thiepval came under threat as Mouquet Farm was captured.

One erudite soldier participant in these circumstances during the middle part of the Somme battles was Edmund Blunden. His incomparable book, *Undertones of War*, is a memorable and illuminating insight into the life of an officer serving with an infantry battalion, the 11th Royal Sussex, during the Great War. A significant portion of that book deals in detail with the events which unfolded around the Schwaben Redoubt north of Thiepval during the autumn of 1916. Blunden's work is fine literature, poetry and a magnificently sensitive evocation of the sights, sounds and terrors which abounded in Thiepval at that time. Often, within the awfulness which pervaded all, Blunden was able to capture the moments of humour and human warmth which made life more bearable for the combatants. Throughout his work a critical eye is cast towards the high command's concept of the 'offensive spirit'. Yet Blunden was a man who did not shirk his duty, but he was sensible and sensitive enough to know that it need not have been this way.

His arrival in the British trench system in the autumnal shadows of

Ruins of Flers Village. Today Flers' population are preoccupied with the business of agricultural life and few visitors come here to dwell upon its significance in the history of modern warfare.

The Butte de Warlencourt. *(opposite)*

The fag end of the battle. Worn out and crushed of the desire to carry on, the conflict's impetus finally gave out here on the road from Albert to Bapaume. This was the furthest point of advance and marks the termination of four and a half months of enormously costly attrition. By that stage in November the weather had turned the landscape into an impassable morass of mud. Over that loathsome scene the white chalk spoil of the Butte de Warlencourt gleamed with a spiteful eye. Today it has acquired a veneer of foliage and greenery which belies its once uncompromising dominance over the last vestiges of the 1916 Battle of the Somme.

The emptiness of this scene eloquently describes the sense of exhaustion and loss which the Battles of the Somme had induced. The poignancy of this place lies in the fact that having defended it with such passion and resilience the German army were soon to make a voluntary withdrawal, in the spring of 1917, with the imperative intention of shortening their positions, thus saving on the manpower required to hold those lines. In that single fact is the most telling testimony to the success of the British troop's efforts upon this lonely battlefield.

Not surprising then, but nevertheless still remarkable, that within months of this position being reached the surviving soldiers and their command were able to galvanise their spirit and resources into conducting three major battles during the following year, those at Arras, Ypres and Cambrai.

Thiepval was as part of an officers' reconnaissance party in early September. Having left his platoons at Martinsart Wood he passed into Aveluy Wood which 'is strangely uninhabited; the moss is rimy, its red leaves make a carpet not a thread less fine than those in King's houses.' Through the wood and along the railway line, where he expected to see the 2.30 for Albert at any

As at Flers, tanks were deployed during the capture of Thiepval in September 1916. The bleak photograph below shows 'the old British system looking up towards lofty Thiepval.'

moment, Blunden looked out towards Authuille across the Ancre.

'A trolley-line crosses, too, but disjointedly: disjointedness now dominates the picture. When we have passed the last muddy pool and derailed truck, we come into a maze of trenches, disjointed indeed; once, plainly, of nice architecture and decoration, now a muddle of torn wire netting and twisted rails, of useless signboards, of foul soaked holes and huge humps - the old British system looking up towards lofty Thiepval.'

Their destination was a dugout in Thiepval Wood. As they make their way up,

Suzanne. (opposite)

The village of Suzanne lies on the banks of the River Somme. Geographically that is immediately south of the area held by the 30th Division prior to their attacks towards Montauban on 1 July 1916. On the British front line Maricourt was the 30th Division's own front line village facing Montauban. But Maricourt's proximity to the forward trenches made it untenable as a billet for the troops. Suzanne fitted the bill. On the river banks, immediately south of the village, was a magnificent chateau. Throughout the preparations for the Big Push the chateau was put to use as a Brigade headquarters. However, the ornate buildings were beyond the range of heavy artillery and the staff officers shared the same privations as the ordinary soldiers who were billeted in the simple village houses. Dug-outs abounded and the cellars were fortified to make them proof against all but a direct hit.

There are two cemeteries adjacent to Suzanne. One, the Suzanne Communal Cemetery Extension, started by the 5th Division who came here in the autumn of 1915, was constructed adjacent to the village's own cemetery plot. The arrival of the Pals units of the 30th Division, in early 1916, saw a rapid expansion of the cemetery and a very large number of the earliest casualties from the Manchester and Liverpool Pals are buried here. The road past this cemetery led towards the front line positions at Carnoy and many reliefs and wiring parties would have marched past here in the dead of night, towards the glare of the Very lights and rockets, saddened to see the numbers of their Pals in the growing cemetery.

The other cemetery, Suzanne Military, is very different in character. This cemetery encompasses a great range of military units and dates of death. There is little logical order to this burial ground which was used almost as an overspill. Bodies found during postwar battlefield clearances were brought here to refill the graves of French soldiers whose bodies were exhumed to be taken to their National Cemeteries near Albert or Etinehem.

'shell after shell hisses past our heads into the inundations of the Ancre, below this shoulder of brown earth, lifting as high as the hill wild sputtering founts of foam and mud. God! Golly! The next salvo - and here's that dugout. A stained face stares out. 'I shouldn't stand there, if I were you: come in.' 'No, I'm all right: don't want to be in the

way.' 'Come in, blast you; just had two men killed where you are.'
For some weeks Blunden's battalion was engaged in the thick of the fighting at Thiepval and in positions overlooking Grandcourt. His survival seemed almost miraculous when all around was devastation and death.

By 26 September Thiepval finally fell to the 18th Division, and within days most of the ridge and high ground above Grandcourt had also fallen.

'.....this was Stuff Trench; three feet deep, corpses under foot, corpses on the parapet. He [Geoffrey Salter] told us, while shell after

Soon after 1 July the collection of paybooks and identification became a priority before the process of burial created a multitude of cemeteries whose existence marks the tragedy of this day from Gommecourt to Montauban.

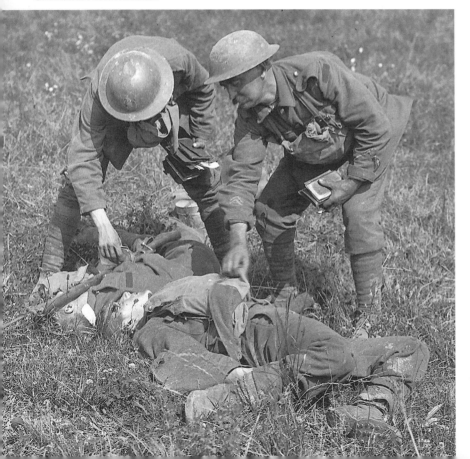

shell slipped in crescendo wailing into the vibrating ground, that his brother had been killed, and he had buried him; Doogan had been wounded, gone downstairs into one of the dugout shafts after hours of sweat, and a shell had come downstairs to finish him...'

With the benefit of retrospective vision it seems incredible that, on 1 July, almost three months earlier, the Salford Pals had been expected to secure Thiepval village and Mouquet Farm within hours of the start of the Great Push. By the end of September all the dominant high ground which had faced Kitchener's army on 1 July was now in British hands.

Blunden's departure from this area, which had clearly made a huge impact upon him, was also beautifully recorded. In his testimony Blunden recalled how, below Thiepval on that day,

'A Highland unit was filing into the line. At the ration-party's

Thiepval. (opposite)
The Thiepval Memorial to the Missing is simply the names. They are names of men who died namelessly. Denied the dignity of a burial amongst their known comrades. These are the men who were swept away by the callous detonation of a nearby shell, or those whose bodies were covered within some lousy dug-out swamped by shellfire or rotted in No Man's Land after another in the seemingly unending sequence of attacks.

Some were later found - their faces obliterated by time or the awfulness of war. They lie under the many headstones whose only epitaph is that the man below is 'Known unto God'. A few whose names appear on these pillars have since been found, sometimes eighty years on, their bodies made known again by documentation and identity discs. For those few the long years identified only as 'missing' has ended. Those men's names now appear twice, once upon the Thiepval Memorial to the Missing and again on a newly erected headstone.

The choice of Thiepval has always struck me as an inspired one. All who knew this place at the fag end of 1916 thought of it as evil. Now it is the first choice of many thousands of visitors every year, people who seek inspiration and challenge from its bold statement of the cost of warfare. It is impossible to come here and not feel the names call out to you, challenging you to think of war as something tenable, something you dare wage in future without thinking of what has been done in its name here upon the Somme.

Many of the names recorded here are those men with whom Edmund Blunden had 'in the golden dusty summer tramped down into the verdant valley'. Kitchener's New Armies. The Thiepval Memorial to the Missing is as much their marker on this planet as any other place I know. Thousands are still fondly remembered by their families across the world. It is an easy matter to consult the Commonwealth War Graves Commission's records. Here you will find many names. One such was Private Robert Stark, G/7190, 7th Battalion, The Queen's (Royal West Surrey Regiment) who died here at Thiepval on Thursday 28 September 1916, aged 23. These men are the story.

rendezvous below Thiepval, our hearty Quartermaster Swain was with his transport, and in particular he was guarding, with all the skill of years of suspicion and incident, our issue of rum. When he called at headquarters presently, he was distressed, and his 'eyes were wild.' Two jars of rum had been lifted under his very nose by the infallible Jocks. It was a feat of arms indeed, but poor Swain felt his occupation was gone.'

But now it was the battalion's chance to leave. It was not the same men who had arrived but their joy at going from Thiepval was unconfined. The

'...limbers were soon more than brimful, and we hustled down through Authuille and over Black Horse Bridge, 'for ever and ever.' The battalion was on the roadside ready to march, and amid humorous and artful glances we fell in. Lancashire Dump in the verge of Aveluy Wood, and the old French fingerposts and notices, and the mossy clear places between the trees, and the straight, damp, firm highway, good-bye to you all; there in the marsh the wild duck and moorcock noise, and farther behind one hears the stinging lash of shells in the swamp, but we are marching. Not the same 'we' who in the golden dusty summer tramped down into the verdant valley, even then a haunt of every leafy spirit and the blue-eyed ephydriads, now Nature's slimy wound with spikes of blackened bone.....'

Taking advantage, the British now pressed grimly forward. During October both the width and depth of British advances increased. On some days those advances were measured by hundreds of yards. Such figures seem pitiful today, but in the context of 1916 they were significant. At the start of the last week in October the weather began to break up. This would have far-reaching consequences, not least at Verdun where the French had finally gained the advantage. In that forsaken place French and German troops had now been locked together for eight months.

By 7 November the British advance towards Bapaume effectively came to a halt. They had reached the Butte de Warlencourt. This heap of mining spoil, originally thrown up during the Roman occupation of Gaul, had been fought over during the Franco-Prussian war and now formed a pronounced landmark against which the British progress could be measured. It was some six and a half miles from the original British lines below La Boisselle, from which the Tommies had launched their attack along this road four and a half months previously.

Even then, as autumn turned into a bitter, relentless, sodden wind which lashed the troops, all was not done. In a last throw the British army launched the Battle of the Ancre proper, sometimes regarded as the fourth phase of the Battle of the Somme. On 13 November the villages of St.Pierre Division and Beaumont Hamel were captured. The following day Beaucourt-sur-Ancre fell. By 18 November the last guttering flickers of life in the Somme campaign ebbed away in front of Grandcourt village in the Ancre valley. The earth's surface within that valley was a brutal parody of its pre-war appearance. Shellfire had reduced the low-lying ground to a moonscape of waterlogged shellholes. The Ancre's waters had flowed through its shattered embankments into the surrounding terrain where they had lodged in a frozen wasteland. Nothing of man's previous tenancy here remained intact. Until this moment, in late 1916, nothing that the British army had endured had been worse than this terrible place.

The human costs were enormous. Total German casualties on the Somme were variously estimated at between 660,000 to 680,000. The combined British

Dive Copse Military Cemetery. *(opposite)*

This is not a place to stand alone on a cold winter's afternoon. As short daylight dwindles, the sense of desolation and heartbreak which pervades this place is almost tangible. Yet, in summer the place is transformed by the heat of day and the ubiquitous skylark's song overhead. No matter how far from the beaten track, and few come to visit this place, the work of the Commonwealth War Graves Commission's gardeners goes on unrelentingly.

Dive Copse Military Cemetery stands isolated on the Morlancourt Ridge, between the two rivers whose courses so influenced the Battles of the Somme. Throughout the long months of the 1916 conflict, all along the Ancre valley to the north and within the Somme valley to the south, numerous Main Dressing Stations gave succour to the wounded. Here were water, morphia and occasional quiet words of encouragement from the clergy whose military wing was so vital to sustaining wounded men's spirits. Such words would have been welcome - this MDS is many miles behind the front lines and the soldiers arriving here had already suffered a terrible and desperately uncomfortable journey, often with little more than a hastily applied Field Dressing to staunch the flows of blood from a gaping wound. The station here was named after the officer who ran the facility. His work was just one small cog in an enormous enterprise. Wounded men were collected in posts within the forward trenches and moved back through a system of Advanced and Main Dressing Stations until they could be placed on hospital trains bound for 'Blighty', or taken to the surgical facilities and proper nursing care of a Casualty Clearing Station.

At each stage difficult decisions were made, filtering those whose wounds gave no chance of survival. Amongst the low walls, here at Dive Copse, are numerous men who 'Died of Wounds'. Their names are, in almost every case, known. Their collective and personal suffering can never be underestimated.

and French in the region of 630,000 casualties. It is a measure of the battle's outcome that when the words were written about the army saying that it 'had been fought to a standstill and was utterly worn out' they were penned by Ludendorff rather than Haig.

However, war was not yet finished with these devastated villages and their shell ravaged landscapes. In the spring of 1918 a German offensive, mounted as a last-ditch attempt to turn the tide of war, swept through before being halted west of Albert. Later that year the British final advance brought renewed fighting and many British cemeteries on the Somme battlefield therefore contain graves from 1915 through each consecutive year to late 1918.

CHAPTER FIVE

YPRES 1

The Salient

The winter of 1916/17 was exceptionally severe, commencing with a period of drenching rain which left the trenches flooded with mud and oily, evil-smelling opaque fluids. January and February of 1917 then saw weeks of continual frost clawing at the resolve of troops within the trenches. Ground was metamorphosed into impenetrably hard rock, making the preparation of new trenches and the repair of damaged stretches an insurmountably severe test of strength and resolve. Meteorological records show this as the coldest winter since 1880. In Germany the issue of her domestic morale was giving rise to concern. Food supplies were erratic, their distribution unfair. After the massive losses of manpower incurred during Verdun, The Somme and the Brusilov offensive, Germany turned to the seemingly attractive option of unrestricted submarine warfare. Events proved this to be a catastrophic misjudgement on Germany's part, leaving the way open for the inevitable entry of American manpower and economic resources.

In that context it is illuminating to look at the losses of British shipping during 1917. It is all too easy, because of the ready availability of film from the Second World War, to imagine that submarines were only then deployed in large numbers. In fact the undersea conflict of the Great War was of enormous threat to British interests, especially so after 31 January 1917, when Germany took the decision to wage unrestricted submarine warfare on allied vessels and ships supplying those countries.

Month.	British Merchant. ship losses:	Tonnage lost.
January	49	153,899
February	105	310,868
March	127	352,344
April	169	526,447
May	122	345,293
June	122	398,773
July	99	359,539

August	91	331,370
September	78	186,647
October	86	261,873
November	64	175,194
December	85	257,807

[Source: *Passchendaele in Perspective*. Ed P.Liddle.]

But here, east of Ypres, the struggle ground on. By the summer of 1917 the Ypres Salient had figured prominently in the Great War's most critical events for almost three years. Within the first few months of war, during the late autumn of 1914, villages like Gheluvelt, Langemarck and Hooge had become bywords for perpetual brutality. The contest for ascendancy in the Ypres area went on ceaselessly. By December 1914 the town had taken on an emotional significance far beyond its strategic importance. And above all this perpetual horror, on a ridge which always eluded the British troops below, stood a sequence of villages whose names were destined for immortality in the Great War's grim legend of murderous holes; Zonnebeke, Gravenstafel, Poelcappelle, Westroozebeke. But most significant, occupying the most prominent part of the ridge, was the village of Passchendaele.

Ever since the end of the war Passchendaele's name has always exerted a fascination upon succeeding generations not only because of the genuinely horrible battle which fetched up within its wreckage by November 1917, but also because of the unusual and poetic juxtaposition of its English pronunciation – 'passion dale'. The name is evocative of both Christ's suffering and an unspoken aura of tranquillity. Nothing could have been further from the crude reality of battle here in 1917.

But before the ultimate degradation of war was unleashed here in 1917 much had happened, east of Ypres, in the preceding three years. In the first weeks of war the great wheeling 'right hook' which was the Schlieffen Plan brought German troops through Belgium and into north-eastern France in the search for every opportunity to outflank, divide and defeat the French and British armies. That relatively small British Expeditionary Force had already fought at the Battles of Mons (23 August), Le Cateau (26 August) and The Marne (6-10 September). By October 1914 the German army was seeking desperately to outflank the British and was advancing rapidly towards the Belgian coastline, marking the start of the Battle of Flanders. Now the great weight of German force was thrown against the combined French, Belgian and British forces in the area. On 19th October 1914 the First Battle of Ypres began. The following day Poelcappelle fell to the German troops; on the 22nd Langemarck; on the 24th Polygon Wood. All were names which would figure again bleakly during the immense struggle which the Third Battle of Ypres became in the autumn of 1917. All the while the German stranglehold was closing around the north-east and east of Ypres. By 31st October 1914 the situation was critical. That day the Germans captured Gheluvelt and threatened to sever the British lines, but the situation was saved by a remarkable counter attack by the 2nd Worcesters inspired by Brigadier General FitzClarence VC, of the 1st Guards Brigade. The following day the Germans overran the villages of Messines, Hollebeke and Wytschaete, south and south-east of Ypres, to complete their dominance over the town from

The spires of distant Ypres. (opposite)
The spires and towers which rise from the urbane environment of Ypres have seen more than their fair share of bloodletting. During four years of the Great War this place witnessed the most tense and fluctuating struggle whose fortunes ebbed and flowed within sight of these historic buildings. Once these fields, which today lay peaceful siege to the town, echoed to the hatred of a thousand artillery pieces. In the trenches which latticed these meadows men wretched daily at the pervading stench of decay which infiltrated every pore of their being. This was where the essence of twentieth century war was distilled into the most infamous cocktail of stubbornly inhuman immobility, presided over by the unremitting mechanisms of modern technology waging war.

Today the Cloth Hall and the cathedral of St. Martin have been lovingly recrafted to recreate their medieval, religious and commercial splendour. Ypres has become a relaxed and comfortable town, satisfied with its affluence and at peace with its extraordinary place in the twentieth century's history. Many of the surrounding buildings have been rebuilt in the solid Flemish style and brickwork whose origins are founded in the prosperity of this otherwise unremarkable corner of Belgium.

At the centre of the town the finest of those restored buildings, the Cloth Hall, now plays host to a unique museum whose arcane portrayal of the war gives rise to perpetual debate about the merits of such representations of the conflict. Through its doors and along the nearby streets and ramparts flow an unending stream of visitors. In the early twenties those visitors included both royalty and the impoverished, between whom The Salient's appetite for death made no distinction. Soldiers, saying goodbye to comrades left forever in Ypres, came here in their thousands. Further thousands upon thousands of wives, daughters, sweethearts and children came to tend the forest of graves or visit the scene where some soul was swept away into the category of the missing. Today the descendants are here in numbers still. Some of those people would describe their presence here as a pilgrimage. Others are simply curious at the story of twentieth century warfare. Some are here on school business. A few are maintaining an ongoing commitment to the dead, and the desire to ensure that they shall not be forgotten.

higher ground. By the middle of the month of November the fighting was losing impetus. Flooding, rain and enervation meant that the nature of warfare settled into a static contest.

Now only the intermittent rhythms of the gunners disturbed the exhausted peace.

Those last four hectic months of 1914 had witnessed the devastation of Britain's professional army. The British regular soldiers had earned an extraordinary epithet from the Kaiser using words that he must have uttered with stinging envy: 'That contemptible little army.' Thereafter the surviving men revelled in being known as 'The Old Contemptibles'. In truth it was a fine and appropriate appellation. The men and their officers had shown a contempt for danger, they had looked death in the face and treated that inevitable enemy with scorn. Their forfeit of life and limb had enabled the British to secure the town of Ypres and its routes through to the channel ports.

It would be inappropriate to leave 1914 without mentioning the Christmas Truce. In a war where honourable behaviour, bravery and the spirit of self - sacrifice would gradually become submerged within the mechanical brutality of a modern and industrial war the spontaneous truces which marked 25 December 1914 have a special place. They were an anachronism. And they were also a very visible soldierly snub to the ideal of the 'offensive at all costs'. It was made plain that there would be no repetition.

The new year saw a change in the face of battle here in The Salient[1]. Before summer the character of modern war was changed in perpetuity when the first use of gas was made. The new weapon's indiscriminate and poisoning effects were unpredictable and uncontrollable. Without protection its impact was all consuming. In 1915 no soldier on the battlefield was equipped with anything to shield himself. For those who experienced it the learning curve was steep, always tortured and often deadly.

The first gas attack was launched by the German army on 22 April 1915. It was accompanied by a massive and devastating artillery bombardment on the town of Ypres behind the Allied positions there. This was the commencement of the Second Battle of Ypres which raged throughout the rest of April until the 24 May. By an interesting coincidence this battle began as final preparations were being made for the landings at Gallipoli, due three days later on 25 April. As at Gallipoli the British had cause to be grateful to the determination of her Empire troops. The potentially disastrous breach in the lines at Ypres was rectified by the intervention of Canadian troops whose memorial stands as a stark pointer towards the new and inhumane practices of war which would thereafter distinguish the 20th century. (See map page 107)

Thus, within the space of six months two epic defensive battles had been fought by the British army east of Ypres. Throughout the subsequent two years, before the great battles for Messines and Passchendaele, life in The Salient continued to be immensely difficult. Most men approached the town of Ypres with trepidation - its reputation having preceded their arrival. Battalions of infantry would march in from the direction of Poperinghe, the British railhead to the Ypres area. At night the flickering colours of flares, the clangour of each shell's detonation and the steady rattle of nervous machine guns meant that the place was never still. In most areas The Salient's trenches were cut into heavy soils whose drainage properties left much to be desired. In winter the conditions underfoot were atrocious. Few men could withstand the strain of front-line conditions for long, especially here at Ypres, and it was necessary to rotate units within each Division and Brigade in and out of the

Three Salford Pals pictured in the spring of 1917, make up a four-man patrol (the fourth being the photographer) about to go into No Man's Land.

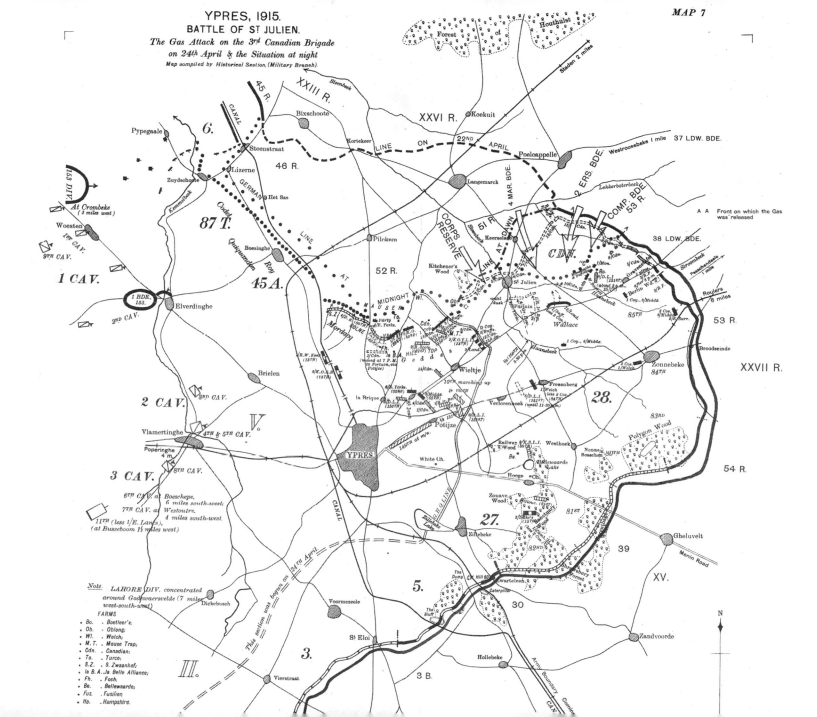

YPRES, 1915.
BATTLE OF ST. JULIEN.
The Gas Attack on the 3rd Canadian Brigade
on 24th April & the Situation at night
Map compiled by Historical Section, (Military Branch).

MAP 7

Note: LAHORE DIV. concentrated
around Godewaersvelde (7 miles
west-south-west)

FARMS

- Bo. . Boetleer's;
- Ob. . Oblong;
- Wl. . Welch;
- M.T. . Mouse Trap;
- Cdn. . Canadian;
- To. . Turco;
- S.Z. . S. Zwaanhof;
- la B.A..la Belle Alliance;
- Fh. . Foch;
- Be. . Bellewaarde;
- Fus. . Fusilien;
- Ha. . Hampshire.

A A Front on which the Gas
was released

Gheluvelt. *(above)*

The remarkable château at Gheluvelt is one of the very few buildings within the Ypres area which retains most of its prewar structure. The area is a powerful magnet to many who wish to consider the heroic and violent events which shattered the peace in this immediate vicinity. It was here, during the First Battle of Ypres on 31 October 1914, that the 2nd Battalion of the Worcester Regiment counter-attacked the advancing Bavarian units and then retook the village of Gheluvelt. Their actions that day, as part of the 1st Division's stand, secured the Menin Road and enabled the British to establish a more secure defence in front of Ypres. Four years later, as the war's end approached during late September 1918, the château and the village were again the scene of intense fighting as British troops fought to recapture this ground. Yet throughout this interminable torture almost all the walls of the chateau remained upright enabling later reconstruction work to recreate the ambience and appearance of its prewar nobility.

The Menin Gate. *(opposite)*

There are numerous memorials to the missing. The Western Front, with its interminable immovability, necessarily gave rise to many thousands of such losses. In that context the Menin Gate memorial is nothing different. It should not stir the emotions any more than the lonely and unvisited cemeteries north of Arras – but it does.

The memorial was inaugurated on 27 July 1927. We know that it is inscribed with the names of 54,896 missing. We know that a further 35,000, killed after 15 August 1917, are recorded at Tyne Cot. We know that the location of this memorial, at that very place where so many men marched east to their pitiable destiny, is enormously evocative. But why it should inspire such a tangible sense of solemnity and warmth, in such depth, is difficult to understand.

Like its equivalent upon the Somme, at Thiepval, the Menin Gate is not a beautiful structure. Nor was it meant to be. These structures were, and continue to be, functional. However, the two are very different in nature. Thiepval is angular, brutally bleak and challenging. By contrast the Menin Gate is bold and mature, a confident statement of style and the grandeur of Empire – perversely created at that time when Empire had ceased to be a relevant or meaningful description of British influence. In some respects the Menin Gate, hemmed in within Ypres' comfortable urbanity, is a far more intimate place than Thiepval. Nevertheless, the edifice of the archway had to be sufficiently large to carry the names. Put simply, this is where the missing, quite tangibly, are. However, the sheer numbers of those missing defied the best intentions and the multitudes of epithets soar to heights where their identification is impossible for any but the most acute vision. Perhaps that is part of the gate's timeless appeal.

Whatever you think of the commemoration of sacrifice on this scale it is scarcely possible that anyone who visits this place for the first time will fail to be moved. True, there are some who arrive unprepared, unknowing and uncaring, and who pass through with little thought for what is revealed here. They leave no mark and learn nought. There are others who cannot shake off the past and who come here to redeem themselves a little, hoping that a fragment of some imagined better past will rub off upon them here. There are those who simply want to remember and dwell upon their thoughts of how the Great War has manipulated the soul of the twentieth century. There are school parties and groups from every corner of the earth. There are Americans and Japanese, Dutch, Germans, Italians, Irish, Scots, Welsh and English. There are those who are just passing through.

At the end of the day, when the business of this small town has been concluded, the local fire-brigade staff come here to play The Last Post. They have done it with love and without break or payment, apart from the years of the Second World War, for every night of every year since 11 November 1929. Those men's labour is immensely significant for all who know a little of the war's history. The conjunction of the brief ceremony and the backdrop of 'Those nameless names' is always inspirational. I have never yet heard those sonorous notes without knowing that a tear has welled within my eyes.

front lines as quickly as possible. All such reliefs and supply work, entrenchment and repair was undertaken at night. In the darkness patrols wrestled for dominance of No Man's Land and sought to capture prisoners for identification and interrogation. In isolated listening posts small groups of men huddled in search of some scrap of intelligence. Sullen parties of tense soldiers stretched interminable miles of cruelly barbed wire in front of their lines each night, waiting for the chance illumination of a flare to reveal them to waiting gunners. And the gunners of each side sought each other and the soft infantry targets ceaselessly. Those gunners' legacies were everywhere. The Salient pumped a steady stream of casualties back to Poperinghe. Cemeteries grew with monotonous, predictable certainty.

Throughout 1916 there was no respite to the steady attrition which characterised death in The Salient. But the focus of British strategic attention that year was drawn down to the Somme battlefield. On the technological battlefield Germany's opponents showed that they were not reluctant to engage in other forms of unrestricted warfare. The British Special Brigade, a seemingly innocuous euphemism for gas specialists, had refined their systems speedily after that first German gas attack in 1915. Initially chlorine was used, soon followed by phosgene in December of 1915. In 1917 the Ypres sector gave a casual name to another gas, first used here in that year, called dichlorodiethyl sulphide or mustard gas – 'Yperite' to the uninitiated! In reality many soldiers from both sides of No Man's Land were accustomed to

Passchendaele 17 August. A plank road winds past a camouflaged British artillery position under German counter battery fire. By the close of 1917 almost every vestige of life had been torn away from the landscape east of Ypres.

The Facade of the Cloth Hall. (opposite)

For over 600 years this magnificent edifice has hidden the intricacies of the European cloth trade from prying eyes. Adjacent to the hall lies a vast square, the Grote Markt, once the Grande Place, where food stalls, clothing merchants, street vendors, entertainers and travellers mingled for many hundreds of years at this vital crossroads which lies en route for the channel ports. Even today the Cloth Hall takes it place both at the centre and heart of Ypres which has, because of its trade and wealth, been besieged on a number of occasions. A century before the Great War, as Napoleon's denouement at Waterloo drew near, the British were here in occupation of the town.

However, by 1914 the town of Ypres no longer held centre stage in the woollen cloth trade. Lancashire cotton and Yorkshire woollens had superseded its place. The city was already set upon accepting a declining role when war came again in late 1914. The first shells struck in November. Progressively the consequential fires and further shell damage reduced the building to a crumbling and deeply pocked travesty of its former glory. It is possible to find many of those vast stones, which make up the lower strata of this building, still scarred by shellfire.

The reconstruction of the façade took almost forty years, an epic of endurance completed by stonemasons in 1962. Apart from the museum the hall today plays host to many of Ypres' civic offices. Immediately behind the Cloth Hall is St. Martin's Cathedral, more properly the spiritual centre of the town, but whose rather drab appearance is overshadowed by the exuberant commercialism and deep decorative relief of the Cloth Hall's exterior.

London Scottish Memorial – the Messines to Wytschaete Road.

What distinguishes this memorial, one of many hundreds of similar structures across the length and breadth of the Western Front, is that it denotes a significant change in the character of units used by the British Army. Before the Great War the Territorial Army were 'Saturday Night' soldiers who had volunteered for home service. Such an arrangement would release regular troops in the event of a significant emergency. The Great War immediately overwhelmed such futile and romantic distinctions with its overwhelming need for men in France and Flanders. Soon after the war's outbreak pressure was brought to bear on those Territorials to serve abroad and almost to a man they volunteered for such duty. At Gallipoli many were destined to fight with great determination during the summer of 1915, but it was here, just north of Messines, that the very first Territorial unit to see action abroad was deployed. They were the London Scottish who, before the war, had been a group of exiles in the capital. Unlike their part-time comrades who had the benefit of months of training in Egypt before being sent into the cauldron of battle at Gallipoli, the London Scottish were in no real way prepared for the exigencies of war between professional troops. Their first foray was marked by enormous bravery but utter naivete along the Messines Ridge. The battalion was crippled by terrible losses. Of seven hundred and fifty who went in, more than three hundred became casualties on 31 October 1914: Ypres Day.

The Canadian Memorial at Vancouver Corner.

This is one of the most visible and starkly poignant places on the Ypres battlefields. It records the passage into modernity of indiscriminate poisoning gases and, during that attack, the bravery of Canadian soldiers who were able, almost by sheer force of their willpower, to resist its debilitating and demoralising effects. The Canadian presence here, and their soldiers' willingness to fight on the far side of the Atlantic Ocean for something which they regarded as right and proper, brought those men into something which had until 1915 been beyond the experience of all men.

The crossroads at Vancouver is overseen by the sorrowing figure of an infantryman. Many who see the sculpture are moved by the attitude of prayer into which the man has been crafted. His hands rest upon his reversed rifle, symbolic of the laying down of arms in search of peace. In many ways the imagery is an unusually modern and clean means to mark such a dark episode in man's evolving history. The inscription reads simply that:

'This column marks the battlefield where 18,000 Canadians on the British left withstood the first German gas attacks the 22-24 April 1915. 2000 fell and lie buried nearby.'

gas and the use of the rapidly evolving protective equipment and respirators. However, the blistering and slow-acting mustard gas took a prolonged time to disperse following its deployment as part of a barrage of artillery shells. To the unwary, or those not forewarned, the presence of mustard gas in shell holes and low-lying ground was capable of devastating and overwhelming a man's respiratory system within moments. It was just another trying addition to the soldier's experience of The Salient.

1917 makes a good case to be thought of as one of the most significant years of the 20th Century. This year three major offensive battles were destined to be fought by the British; Arras, Messines-Passchendaele and Cambrai. All would be dramatically different in nature. Of the three Messines-Passchendaele was by far the most important. It was undertaken with the intent of freeing the Belgian coast and the channel of the menace of U-boats and minelayers operating from Ostend, Zeebrugge and Bruges. Its genesis grew amidst developing concerns about the French army's willingness to carry on in the face of her ever-mounting casualties. As on the Somme the British army's willingness to support and aid her Entente partner would be tested to the very limit of her soldiers' endurance.

Water. The ubiquitous enemy of every man at Ypres. In winter its presence in every hollow threatened illness, exposure and a constant sapping of energy. To the miners the presence of water was disastrous and pumping was a constant corollary to the driving of new subterranean works.

The Choice of Messines Ridge and Passchendaele.

The Battle of Messines Ridge was fought during the second week of June 1917. It was something of an object lesson, within the chequered military history of the Great War, in how to fight and win a limited engagement, achieving defined objectives, before making the decision to stop the battle quickly.

How then did this success drift into the tragedy of Passchendaele?

The planning for the Messines-Paschendaele campaign had been in train for many months. Since 1915 extensive tunnelling work beneath the Messines Ridge had been undertaken by the British. Vast quantities of explosives had been placed in galleries some 30-40 metres below the German trenches[2]. Since the first weeks of 1916 Haig had been convinced that the capture of the Belgian coastline would be a far more effective ploy than any combined Franco-British offensive on the Somme during 1916. Apart from purely military matters, the prospect of settling the submarine threat, which emanated from that coastline, appealed greatly. Because of the inundation of much land north of Ypres Haig felt that it would be necessary to push east

---

2. Twenty-four mines in total. Three were not fired and two were lost to geological and water-pumping problems.

from Ypres itself. The consequence of that intention was that the Gheluvelt Plateau and the Messines Ridge, lost during the 1915 battle, would both have to be recaptured in order to allow troops the chance of fighting their way up to and past Passchendaele, Westroozebeke and Staden without the prospect of being enfiladed by observed artillery fire from the relatively higher ground of the Gheluvelt Plateau and the Messines Ridge.

Once the Somme campaign had taken on its own momentum in 1916 it became clear that Messines – Passchendaele was a non-starter that year. Resources were over stretched. Therefore arrangements were made to try and preserve the structure and secrecy of the mine tunnels beneath Messines through the winter.

By the end of 1916 both the British Government and the French Commander-in-Chief were in agreement with Haig that the principal military aim of campaigning in 1917 should be the expulsion of German forces from the Belgian coastal ports of Ostend and Zeebrugge. This would follow a series of wearing-down or attritional battles to weaken German resolve. Great debate centred around the nature of the coastal assault, eastwards from Nieuport, and the possibility of using a naval force to land troops further east. Unfortunately this debate was overtaken by the momentous changes which swept through the French command structure during December. Joffre, the long standing Commander-in-Chief, was replaced by General Nivelle, a confident and autocratic man who felt able to deliver a decisive defeat upon

Shrapnel Corner. (opposite)

The naive use of everyday language to describe a place of great danger to the soldiers who frequently crossed these places always makes me smile inwardly. The use of familiar terms in a bleak context seems to encompass both a sense of perspective and black humour with a knowledge of how fragile and temporary life could be here in The Salient. Shrapnel Corner was a devilishly difficult place, just south of the Lille Gate en route for 'Whitesheet'. It was constantly shelled throughout the war years at long range by guns seeking opportune targets amongst the slothful or unwary. The signs deployed here today by the Commonwealth War Graves Commission, point to numerous nearby cemeteries where those who were too slow or ill-informed are buried in profligate numbers.

Other places within The Salient acquired a similar or even greater degree of notoriety. Principal amongst those was Hellfire Corner on the Menin Road. Both Hellfire Corner and Shrapnel Corner were distinguished by features which made the registration of German artillery a simple task. At both places a road junction was itself crossed by a railway line. At Hellfire Corner that was the Ypres to Roeselaere line. Here at Shrapnel Corner it was the Ypres to Comines line.

the Germans by the massive deployment of French forces and an increase in the tempo of war.

By January 1917 Haig was seduced by Nivelle's charisma and was actively promoting a policy of co-operation with the imminent French offensive on the Aisne by British attacks on the Vimy – Arras and Ancre fronts. These would be followed by a subsequent and decisive attack eastwards from Ypres. Predictably, and tragically, the Nivelle offensive, begun on 16 April on the Chemin des Dames and in front of Reims, was a disaster. German troops and defences were well prepared. The French army's morale was severely shaken in the face of terrible casualties. Fortunately for Nivelle's broken aspirations the British were already engaged in the Battle of Arras and the continued prosecution of that battle held many German units away from undertaking counter-attacks on the depleted French. During late May and early June large numbers of 'acts of collective indiscipline' amongst French troops broke out. Nivelle was replaced by General Pétain as French Commander-in-Chief. It became clear that any French co-operation in the attempt to break out eastwards from Ypres would be limited. However, Haig was convinced that the need for offensive action was paramount if pressure upon the German army was to be maintained.

Thus, on 7 June, the battle for the capture of Messines Ridge was engaged. It was preceded by three and a half million shells and the detonation of 19 mines. Those mines were placed under the Germans' forward positions in a sequence running from the notorious and much fought over Hill 60, past The Bluff, St.Eloi, Hollandscheschuur Farm, Petit Bois, Spanbroekmolen and across the River Douve towards the German defences just north-east of Ploegsteert Wood. Second Army records show there was 'a gun to every 4.5 yards and 6.5 tons of ammunition to every yard of front attacked.' Estimates

The shattered remains of Ploegsteert Wood.

Railway Wood. *(opposite)*

Those responsible for the burial of the British Army's dead have always taken the greatest care to commemorate that sacrifice of life with as much respect for individuality as is humanly possible. The divisional or unit burials officer often worked under impossible and hugely trying circumstances. In the context of the Great War and its Western Front relatively few bodies were assembled into mass graves. In the case of Railway Wood that sensitivity was taken to its very limits.

Every burial ground is marked by a cross of sacrifice, but here at Railway Wood you will find no evidence of graves. The soldiers commemorated here belonged to the Royal Engineers. These were the tunnellers whose efforts wrought death and destruction at nearby Hooge. Both belligerent parties made extensive use of the skills and courage of such men beneath the elevated ground of Bellewaarde Farm and Hooge Château. It was from the elevated positions surmounting this ridge that German troops had a panoramic vista of the British Army's activities in the Ypres Salient. German control of this place made the Menin Gate almost untenable at times, and made nearby Hellfire Corner the 'Hottest place on Earth'. The British attempts to dislodge those German observers were endless and both sides sought each other in an unremitting subterranean war.

Here at Railway Wood the names of one officer and eleven NCOs and men are commemorated. They were not lost on any one occasion, the underground operations lasted from December 1915 to a week before the opening of the Third Battle of Ypres. What these men have in common is that it proved impossible to recover their bodies to the surface and so they are buried where they died, lost forever in the warren of narrow passageways and slender tunnels which honeycomb the area beneath.

morning of 7 June, was like an earthquake. The impact was felt in Lille and London. Within seconds of the mines' detonations the whole German positions astride the Messines Ridge were saturated with a massive concentration of artillery fire which seemed to set the whole sky and horizon on fire. Nine divisions of the British Army advanced. They found the German troops on the ridge in a state of moral and physical shock and collapse.

By 9.00 am British troops were in positions along the whole length of the Messines – Wytschaete ridge. Casualties had been light – a mere fraction of the 50-60% figures anticipated. Unfortunately heavier casualties now began to be incurred as visible concentrations of British troops on the skyline of the ridge became easy prey to German artillery firing anti-personnel shrapnel. Nevertheless, the artillery's forward observation officers had an unobstructed and distant view into the German rear positions, a luxury not experienced by

Hill 62 trenches and Sanctuary Wood. *(opposite)*

Up Canadalaan or Maple Avenue thousands of visitors arrive throughout all seasons of the year. The vast majority are, I suspect, casual and perhaps a little disinterested after numerous other visits as part of their busy itineraries. What they see here invariably becomes a focus of their day and inserts into their memories a lifelong image of the Great War. Whether that be a true likeness is impossible to say, but it is a powerful one nevertheless.

Surmounting the rise of Hill 62 is another Canadian memorial stone, identical in design to all their other memorials with the exception of that at Vancouver Corner. The stone here commemorates the Canadian Corps' decisive involvement in the Battle of Mount Sorrel which was fought across this high ground and another elevation, Mount Sorrel proper, a little to the south. That battle commenced with a massive German attack on 2 June 1916 whose intent was to capture this high ground, one of the last significant elevations in front of Ypres still in British hands. That assault succeeded and fierce fighting then ensued until 13 June when a brilliant Canadian counter-attack recaptured the hill. This was one of 1916's most significant moments – preceding by just a few days the opening of the Battle of the Somme.

That Canadian memorial is, however, visited by few.

By far the greater numbers come here to visit the incredible cafe and museum which lies alongside Maple Avenue between Hill 62 and Sanctuary Wood cemetery. Inside and behind the cafe is a boisterous and eclectic mixture of artefacts, weapons and relics as well as an improbable collection of 3D or stereoscopic viewers portraying grisly and distressing images of the war. Outside is a stretch of preserved second-line trenches which had been constructed here by the British before the Battle of Mount Sorrel. The fire bays, tunnels, dug-outs and revetting convey a little of the life which soldiers endured within their trenches. I think that everyone who values life and health should come here to view these matters just once in their lifetime. It is many things; unforgettable, tacky, heroic and commercial all in one. But come here you must if only to make up your mind about how this place has come into being.

The British Army's success at Messines suggested that subsequent events during the Passchendaele fighting could have had a different outcome. Here, a British Officer can be seen peering from a newly captured German pillbox aptly named 'Sachsenfeste' which literally translated means Saxon Fort.

of the British casualties likely to be incurred had been calculated at 50% of the leading brigades for the capture of the first intermediate objectives and 60% of the troops engaged in fighting to the first objective proper, east of Messines and Wytschaete. The shock of the mines' explosions, at 3.10 am on the

The power of explosives used in the detonation of the Messines' mines is revealed in the casual devastation of this concrete bunker.

the British in this area since October 1914. At last it was possible for British troops on the western side of the ridge to move in relative safety during daylight hours. During the coming week various smaller actions produced the most advantageous observation positions and the Battle of Messines Ridge was terminated on 14 June.

Once British control of Messines was established the German Army's crucial observation advantage over Ypres was lost.

Hill 60. *(opposite)*

To make sense of Hill 60 requires care and studious preparation. It is one of the most fascinating places on The Salient and retains a powerful atmosphere in a preserved and important battlefield location. To the south are numerous front line battlefield cemeteries such as Woods Cemetery and Chester Farm. This artificial hill was created during the 19th century by spoil thrown up from the construction of an adjacent railway. Little could its constructors have known what anguish their handiwork would bring forth in the years to come. In the featureless environment of the Ypres area such man-made elevations were vital. Similar conflict arose a mile to the south at the Spoilbank on the Ypres – Comines canal.

One of the most experienced guides and historians writing of this hill rightly describes it as 'the centrepiece of the fighting at Ypres'. After the French Army left this area in February 1915 it became part of the British sector and mining operations continued prior to the 5th Division's attack here on 17 April that year. Three weeks later the German Army recaptured this vital observation and it remained in their possession until the Battle of Messines in 1917. Anyone with an eye for topography or the endless interest of detailed maps will know how acutely painful it was for the British Tommy, throughout this period, to look up to this glowering place and to know that all he did could be seen. The sweeping views over much of The Salient which those German observers enjoyed from here meant that offensive mining operations were ubiquitous in this cratered and deeply scarred area. The German occupation of this position was ended with cataclysmic suddenness on 7 June 1917 when one of the immense mines which preceded the Messines assault was detonated here on the south side of the railway line. That mine marked the limit of the left flank of that attack and after the resultant advance the British lines were moved north-eastwards along the railway towards Hollebeke.

Subsequently the hill was recaptured by the Germans in the spring of 1918 and taken back during the last few weeks of war by the British in 1918. The history of the fighting here therefore spans the entirety of the war and involves all of the major western belligerents whose troops served and suffered here at some time during those years.

All of the anticipated objectives had been secured. The German losses in both men and materiel were significant: 144 officers, 7,210 other ranks, 48 artillery pieces, 218 machine guns and 60 trench mortars. German casualties were in the order of 40,000. British casualties during the period of the preliminary movements and the battle itself amounted to less than 25,000.

A very notable victory had been won by the Second Army. This should have been the moment when the Gheluvelt Plateau, near to the Menin road east of Ypres, was captured. However, the coming six weeks of seeming inaction gave the German troops in that area ample time to restore the effectiveness of their defences on the plateau. The British failure to threaten or capture the Gheluvelt positions at the end of the Battle of Messines would lead to many casualties in that area at the start of the now imminent Third Battle of Ypres.

The relatively fine weather of early June ensured the rapid exploitation of success. Here troops advance through the wreckage surrounding Wytschaete.

Messines Ridge. *(opposite)*
There are two settlements which surmount the Messines Ridge. Towards the southern end is Messines village. At the northern end lies Wytschaete, invariably known as 'Whitesheet' to the Tommies. The central and northern aspects of the ridge were captured by two divisions fighting here side by side on 7 June 1917. That collaboration has acquired a deeply symbolic significance as Ulster and Eire struggle today to come to terms with their divided heritage. In the years of the Great War, before this century's political division of Ireland, the 16th (Irish) Division, which comprised many Catholics, and the equivalent 36th (Ulster) Division from the northern counties whose roll call was predominantly Unionist and die-hard protestant, found themselves here on the summit of Messines Ridge. In carrying this place they achieved the first definable and outright British victory since the war's beginning. Of course it is quite possible to argue that both traditions were exploited by the British military authorities throughout the war years, but the events of 7 June 1917 serve as a reminder that the spirit of co-operation served those men well enough more than eighty years ago.

Maps and intelligence have always played a crucial and central role in the ability to win battles. The Great War created a need for utter correctness in that intelligence. Precision quick-firing artillery and, later in the war, aerial bombing meant that specific military targets in known locations could be targeted without the need for direct infantry assault. During the conflict the development of sound-ranging and flash-spotting technology gave impetus to the war between each side's artillery units - the process of counter-battery fire. Maps therefore became as important a tool in the military arsenal as any of the more vaunted weapons of war.

The majority of British military trench maps were reproduced to a scale of 1:10,000. Other scales such as 1:5,000 and 1:20,000 were also employed. Each map had a unique reference number. The maps covered areas from Zeebrugge and Nieuport to St.Quentin and beyond along the Western Front. Each map is further sub divided into large rectangles, themselves sub-divided into squares, 1000 x 1000 yards, each square numbered from 1 to 36. Each numbered square is itself sub-divided into four small squares measuring 500 x 500 yards which are known as a,b,c and d. That is a (to the north-west), b (north-east), c (to the south-west) and d (south-east). Further graduations using tenths or 100ths of each 500 yard axis could be used to give precise locations for the registration of artillery shells or the location of tactically important details such as a pill-box, hidden artillery unit or command post. Thus every position along the Western Front could be identified to within an accuracy of five yards by any officer and that position transmitted and made known to any other person with the command structure. Gunners could then be instructed to fire shells into such positions. Even in periods of poor visibility it was possible for skilled gunners to fire on map co-ordinates with a reasonable chance of success. Maps were thus an essential adjunct to the key element of the Great War, the battle of the artillery.

Today these trench maps are readily available and form an essential ingredient to the success of any walk or tour through the history of the Great War. Try the Imperial War Museum in Lambeth, London, which maintains a stock of such maps, available to the public at very reasonable prices.

Messines village.

Before the Battle of Messines on 7 June 1917 the village lay inside the German-occupied part of the ridge. Gefreiter Adolf Hitler came here, billeted within the crypt of the church. How a chance bullet would have altered history is one of the century's great 'what if' questions. Here German front line trenches were some 800 metres west of the village overlooking the Douve River valley and the British lines towards Wulverghem. On that extraordinary first day of the Battle of Messines amidst the cacophony of the 19 mines and their 1,000,000 pounds of explosive this village was captured by the New Zealand Division. Today the area around Messines provides spectacular walking and wonderful views across the higher ground south of Ypres. Nearby are numerous small British military cemeteries whose names are evocative of places and purposes familiar to the British troops which named these burial grounds, Ration Farm, St. Quentin Cabaret, La Plus Douve Farm.

Compared to Thiepval or Beaumont Hamel on the Somme this place is infrequently visited. No matter. Its history is the equal of anything the Somme has to offer and is all the better without pressure from numerous visitors. Messines is at its best in the early morning of an autumnal day, before the dark soils have lost all vestiges of their summer warmth. As the sun begins to break through the vapour of mist, it transforms this scene into a glorious and invigorating walk from Spanbroekmolen, into Messines and thence through Wulverghem and back to the tranquillity of Lone Tree cemetery.

The Spanbroekmolen Mine Crater.

As with almost any part of lowland Belgium the Messines Ridge is subject to the most complete and instantaneous fluctuations in climate and visibility. I have known ten-mile vistas to be obliterated within minutes by envelopes of low cloud. Rain drives this exposed tract of ground with a bitter chill throughout the autumn and winter months.

I still recall with embarrassment my weak attempts to convince a party of Manchester students that I understood full well where Ypres was whilst stumbling through an impenetrable early morning blanket of Flemish fog here. Wherever that essential companion, my compass, was – I knew not where. In truth I also knew not where Ypres had gone. This can be a bleak place.

Sunshine, however, is capable of transforming everything. On a clear day there are deeply impressive views over inspirational history from this location, clear testimony to the careful siting of the complex of German trenches which once latticed this place and its undeniable importance for observation. Nearby is the fascinating yet intimate cemetery known as Lone Tree. In that often chill corner of Belgium are just eighty-eight men's graves, sixty of whom belong to men of the Royal Irish Rifles, part of the 36th (Ulster) Division which attacked here on the opening day of the Battle of Messines. Many were killed by the falling rock and debris thrown skywards by the detonation of the 91,000 pounds of ammonal used to destroy the German strongpoint formed around the Spanbroekmolen windmill site.

The vast crater, now owned by Toc-H, is more than thirty metres deep, the flooded part being twenty-seven metres to the floor. The area is preserved as a memorial to all who died in the ferocious fighting for this ridge. How many still lie unrecovered within the crater's lips we will never know. Today its reference is simple, The Pool of Peace. Whenever I visit this dark, watery and cavernous hole I cannot help but wonder if 'Pool of Peace' is an appropriate phrase for such a violent place. The senses of detonation and concussion, the all-pervasive tearing and crushing violence is still too prevalent around the Spanbroekmolen Crater. I cannot rid my mind of the imagery and find the act of reflection and contemplation hard in this place.

Maedelstede Farm . *Today the crater at Maedelstede Farm provides opportunities for fishermen and local children to engage in their favorite pastimes. Unlike Spanbroekmolen Mine this place conveys an atmosphere of tranquillity at peace with its surrounding agricultural landscape.*

The Petit Bois and Hollandscheschuur Farm craters.

The village of Wytschaete was protected on its northern and western approaches by a series of woodlands. Two of these woods, the Petit and Grand, saw the detonation of a series of adjacent mines on the first day of the Battle of Messines Ridge, 7 June 1917, in the centre of the positions attacked by the 16th (Irish) Division. At Petit Bois these placid pools are home to fish, water fowl and reeds. Across the length and breadth of the Western Front many such craters had become handy tipping sites for local communities and farmers, many being lost during the 1970s and 1980s to a melange of mattresses, derelict cars and farm refuse. That process was deplorable since numerous craters became war graves containing the remains of many men from all belligerent countries. In the trying aftermath of major assaults mortal remains were often tumbled into any suitable place, with copious quantities of lime to aid decomposition and the production of a sterile environment. Today, here in Belgium, such sites are protected by virtue of their national and historic significance.

A little to the north of the two Petit Bois craters is the site of the three mines which were detonated at Hollandscheschuur Farm in front of the Grand Bois on the northern side of Wytschaete. Looking at these locations today it comes as something of a shock to the untutored eye when realising the terrible human cost of scaling the relatively low height and shallow slopes of the Messines Ridge.

The Ploegsteert Memorial to the Missing.

No place known to local mapmakers as Ploegsteert Wood or Ploegsteertbos could escape the Tommies' affection for anglicising such place names. However, throughout the war years the wood never acquired a familiar or friendly face. Its location, between the high ground of Messines and the low-lying British-held town of Armentières, meant that the densely packed trees took on a considerable tactical importance. The shell shattered trunks, whose roots explored a muddy swamp of legendary and perpetual wetness, were the scene of many serious actions and extensive fighting. There is so much to see that numerous guidebooks have paid intimate attention to the details which still abound here in the depths of the forest. This place has always seemed, to my simple mind, to be a more complete history of the Great War than almost any book which I have read. The story spans the whole period of the conflict and incorporates a diversity of personalities from Winston Churchill to Bruce Bairnsfather. Within the boundaries of the woods there are numerous fortifications, evocatively named farms and intimate cemeteries but the most architecturally grand of the structures is at Hyde Park Corner on the Messines to Armentières road.

Adjacent to the wood is the Ploegsteert Memorial to the Missing as well as two cemeteries, the Berkshire Corner cemetery and an extension to that which partly surrounds the Ploegsteert Memorial. The memorial's panels list the missing from a sequence of battles whose titles are less secure in popular memory; Armentières and Aubers Ridge 1914, Loos and Fromelles 1915, Estaires 1916, Hazebrouck, Scherpenberg and Outtersteene Ridge 1918. The names total 11,447 men.

To mark such tragedy and loss the architecture is of an exquisitely beautiful, though very formal, nature. Endless panels recording the names of the missing are set within a circular domed structure, reminiscent of a classical temple. Outside the pillars are two lions, one defiant, the other contemplative. This is a very traditional British interpretation of a memorial's purpose, set at a very British location on Hyde Park Corner. Yet no more than an hour's drive from here is the unique and uplifting Canadian memorial at Vimy Ridge. I cannot think of two memorials which span a greater divergence in architectural and sculptural inspiration than these two places. Both, for very different reasons, are unforgettably vivid. Both are, in the true sense of the words, memorable memorials.

CHAPTER SIX

YPRES 2

The Third Battle of Ypres–Passchendaele

Of all Ypres' terrible battles this was the one which came to symbolise the cumulative awfulness of The Salient. Whilst the great defensive battles of 1914 and 1915 had stamped the place with the distinction of heroism and the first use of gas, the 1917 battle took on a grotesque momentum of its own, inexorably swallowing manpower at will. In the early years of the war it was volunteer soldiers who came here to Ypres in their thousands, the toughened soldiers of the Regular Army, the 'Saturday Night' soldiers of the Territorials and, during 1916, the Kitchener battalions. But that seemingly inexhaustible supply of enthusiastic men was never going to be capable of winning the war without supplementation from the ranks of

Behind the front lines below Passchendaele Australian troops assemble in trenches amongst the wreckage of Hooge near Clapham Common.

the conscripted. The debate about the morality of using men whose will was against the war will long be discussed and pondered upon, not least by the families whose brief records of an antecedent's service show that he enlisted from 1917 onwards. Such scant knowledge suggests that soldier was conscripted, selected because of his age or marital status, to fight a war as part

This map shows the villages around Ypres from Messines in the south to Langemarck and Poelcapelle to the north of the town.

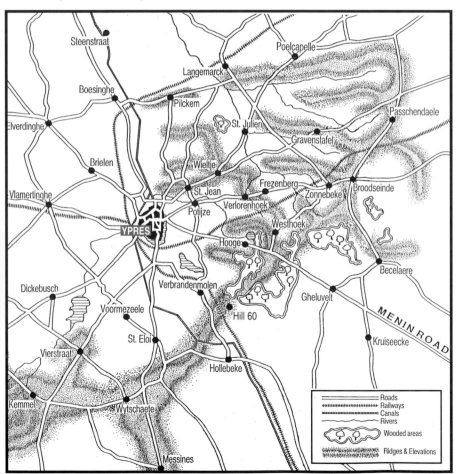

of the armed forces, a process for which, as yet, he had shown little enthusiasm.

Fortunately for the morale of the British Army the men who had survived the Somme battles were a resilient bunch. Many of those citizen soldiers now wore the insignia of rank, thousands having taken promotion to become officers. Many more now regarded themselves as 'old sweats', experienced and battle-hardened men, whose ability to work together, to preserve themselves and their comrades' spirits and to fight was second to none. More than fifty divisions were brought here to take their part in this, the Third Battle of Ypres. Many divisions of Kitchener's Army, such as the 18th and 30th, had already established a reputation for competence and success on the Somme and at Arras earlier in 1917. That proficiency and the ability to recover from Passchendaele's enormous appetite for casualties were put to the supreme test here below that melancholic village.

Once the high ground of the Messines Ridge to the south-east of Ypres had fallen, during the second week of June, the way was open for the development of the campaign to secure a significant tract of territory to the east. The success in early June had the effect of making The Salient far less prominent on its south-eastern aspect where the villages of Messines, Wytschaete and Hollebeke were now secured.

At this stage Haig, the British Commander-in-Chief, was convinced that

German Pill boxes. (opposite)
Concrete. Set in a sea of shell holes and surrounded by the wreckage of military equipment. This is the archetypal image of the Third Battle of Ypres. The image on the right shows the Ziegler or ship bunker on Pilckem Ridge. By 1917 the German Army had long abandoned the concept of competing for every yard of ground. Their mistaken willingness to be brought into attritional battles on the Somme and at Verdun in 1916 had taught a severe lesson. Now their systematic defence was one which depended upon depth into which attackers could be drawn before being shattered by artillery and the interlocking fields of machine-gun fire from numerous pill boxes set in the folds and slopes of the battlefields. Most of these fortifications therefore date from the fighting during 1917 and 1918. These were the scene for numerous heroic actions as men fought with rifle grenades, Lewis guns and small arms to subdue and overwhelm the desperate teams within these blockhouses. Little quarter was given. The men inside knew that in the event they were unable to keep their attackers at bay the inevitable outcome would be a volley of grenades through the gun ports.

Once captured, such defences were turned to the advantage of their captors. Extra concrete was poured to protect the now exposed rear entrance. New purposes were found as the medical and communications teams sought protection from the spectre of artillery which now inevitably sought the known sites of these pill boxes.

the process of 'wearing down and exhausting the enemy' was still of overarching importance. Underlying that was 'the strategic objective of securing the Belgian coast and connecting with the Dutch frontier'. If that could be achieved it would be the most extraordinary success, dealing a potentially terminal blow to Germany's submarine warfare capability and threatening her industrial heartlands. The initial objective would necessarily be the capture of higher ground due east of Ypres.

The phrase 'higher ground' could mislead. The reality was that these low ridges would barely rate a mention in a tourist's guidebook to the South Downs or the Pennines, none at all in any guide to the Highlands of Scotland. But in the context of the Great War, here on the wetlands of the Flanders plain, any prominence which aspired to sixty or more metres above the surrounding levels was of all encompassing military value.

During the weeks which followed the Messines success an enormous logistical exercise was undertaken to gather the necessary men and materiel to this once quiet corner of Belgium. However, the ever-lengthening interval following the capture of Messines Ridge would have serious ramifications.

Many of these concrete fortifications proved imposible to remove in post-war years. Eighty years on they provide shelter for farm animals and a reminder of what evil business war became here on the Salient.

Hooge Crater Cemetery. *(opposite)*
The original buildings and château which once stood on a prominent position astride the Menin Road have long since disappeared. More comprehensively than any other location around Ypres this place was utterly eradicated from the map. Systematic devastation was wrought by both artillery and the subterranean tunnellers whose efforts brought unsuspected oblivion to those unfortunate enough to be here when underground explosives blasted the earth. Every account tells of the fighting's unspeakable ferocity and the sad, torn human detritus which abounded here.

After the war the small burial plot, which had been established in 1918, was chosen as the site for another of those vast assemblies of bodies which were the concentration cemeteries. As you come to this place it is well to remember that the scene's symmetry and beauty disguise the memory of an awfulness which we would do well to avoid in Europe again. Stepping into the cemetery you pass across a symbolic crater before approaching the cross of sacrifice. Those few yards must have held anguish and terrible memories for the survivors of this theatre returning in the early twenties.

Inside is fearful evidence. The bodies brought here were a worldly multitude: Canadians, Australians, New Zealanders, more than 5,000 British soldiers, two from British West Indies. More than half the bodies are, in Kipling's words, 'Known unto God'.

Hindsight suggests that the Passchendaele campaign should have begun contemporaneously with the success at Messines. Unfortunately the need to support the tattered French armies had inserted the decision to launch Messines before the preparation for the Passchendaele offensive was complete.

We should not think of this battle solely as a landlocked contest. Although the Second World War is often regarded as the moment in history when conflict in the air became an integral part of total warfare, the battle for air supremacy in the weeks prior to Third Ypres was of inestimable importance to British hopes for a successful outcome to the fighting. Because of the way in which the Germans had taken advantage of every fold in the ground many

of their defences were not visible to Forward Observation Officers. Without air observation, during periods of inclement weather, British artillery units would be forced to shoot on map co-ordinates and targets revealed by previous air observation and photographic reconnaissance.

Throughout July the work of the Royal Flying Corps in the gaining of supremacy was fought out as a grim battle above the positions below. The work was the very raison d'être of the RFC.

'Artillery observation was well organised and efficient, and aerial

Soldiers watch, with almost casual interest, as shells explode a hundred metres along the Menin Road, east of Ypres.

photography was extensively used, as were strategic aerial reconnaissance and bombing. Contact patrols, flown at perilously low level, monitored the progress and positions of the troops; fighter aircraft harassed the enemy's troops and attacked his aerodromes, which were also bombed by day and night.'

This could so easily describe a scene in the last few years and months of the 20th century. In essence just the speed and instancy of communication has changed! Planes from each side fought out a deadly conflict. The most notable of these was a clash over Polygon Wood, north of Gheluvelt on the Menin Road, involving ninety-four fighter planes at heights between 5,000 and 17,000 feet. Only during the last week of July did it become clear that the German air defences were slowly weakening. By 31 July the British air services on the Western Front included 45 RFC squadrons, 5 Royal Naval Air Service squadrons and sundry other units including 44 Balloon Sections. These squadrons held a total of 858 serviceable aeroplanes.

The battle for the Passchendaele ridge was therefore a very deeply technological struggle. Within that struggle the deployment of air power was a pointer to what would come to be seen, much later in the century, as the first line element of the armed forces. But whatever air power could do in 1917, or 1999 for that matter, the essential element was always going to be the soldier on and in the ground.

Below, dug deeply into his protective pits, camouflaged as part of the terrain, were the artillery's gunners. If those teams of sweating and deafened men could spare a glance skywards it was only for the briefest of moments. These soldiers were engaged in their own game of deadly intent. During early July the British Fifth Army assembled a massive strength of more than 2,100 artillery pieces[1] which were opposed by some 1,500 pieces of German artillery. Throughout the month both sides sought each others' positions in a desperate attempt to gain the sort of ascendancy required to take advantage

of that being fought for in the air. The difficulties faced by the British artillery were immense. Every move was capable of being observed from German positions. Every gun-pit dug had to be drained, made weather-resistant and camouflaged before dawn. Roads and tracks for the ammunition convoys had similarly to be prepared at night and camouflaged by day. Throughout these preparations the men were constantly shelled by both high explosive and gas, including the new mustard gas. Casualties amongst the artillery units and pioneer battalions were high.

Such transparent preparation made the British intentions very clear. The perfect heralding of a forthcoming assault did, however, have one advantage – it drew to the area massive German support, men who otherwise would have been able to capitalise on the failure of the French offensive led by Nivelle to the south. The British assault would thus be opposed by

Horse drawn and various forms of motorised transport take munitions and troops forward during the battle of Pilckem Ridge.

1. 752 Medium and Heavy guns and howitzers as well as 1,098 18 pounder guns and 324 4.5″ howitzers. More than 2,100 pieces of artillery in total.

considerable German strength in depth being massed to the east of Passchendaele. In the forward battle zones the German defences consisted of lightly held front lines, supported by a 'chequered system of strongpoints, to break up and delay an assault, backed by a succession of counter-attack formations ready to recapture any lost ground immediately.' Throughout the period of battle the drawing in of German reserves to the Passchendaele campaign would have a hugely beneficial impact upon the recovery of the French army's morale.

Although the figures of British artillery shell expenditure are often quoted, they are so significant as to be essential to the understanding of what happened in that great bowl of ground below Passchendaele village. In two weeks of preparatory bombardment of German positions, and the first three days of battle, the British gunners fired four million, two hundred and eighty-three thousand, five hundred and fifty shells. Such an incredible weight of firepower was the ultimate expression of the idea that the artillery could conquer whilst the infantry would then subsequently occupy. The figures for comparable bombardments in earlier battles are illuminating:

Battle.	Frontage (miles)	Heavy.	Medium.	Light (field)	Shells expended.
Somme 1916.	14	143	284	1,010	1,732,873
Arras 1917.	13	301	662	1,854	2,687,653
Messines 1917.	9	236	504	1,510	3,258,000
Pass'daele 1917.	15	281	718	2,092	4,283,550

Numbers of artillery pieces (guns):

The consequences of such extravagant shell expenditure was the complete devastation of the traditional Flanders ditches, drains and small streams which were responsible for maintaining the water table below ground level. Whilst this might have been a soluble problem during a fine summer campaign the battle for the Passchendaele ridge was destined to be fought in the most abysmal autumnal and winter weather.

The Third Battle of Ypres commenced on 31 July and continued until the November of that year.

The first troops moved forward, signalling the start of more than three months of continuous fighting, at 3.50 am, sunrise. Initially they made good progress towards and through the German outposts on the Pilckem Ridge, north-east of Ypres, towards Langemarck and into St. Julien where fighting for control of the wreckage continued for three days. Due east of the town, along the Menin Road towards the Gheluvelt Plateau, the German artillery was in better shape and proved capable of dominating the approaches to the plateau. Here carefully orchestrated German barrages fell in the areas of devastated woodland and valleys in which the advancing troops were concentrated and relatively limited progress was achieved. The day therefore belonged to the British (and to the French) on the left of the front attacked, whilst on the right the German defence in depth of the Gheluvelt Plateau had held firm. Casualties were, by comparison with the opening days of the Somme, relatively light. However, what was soon realised was that, because of the German system of defence in depth, most of the casualties were incurred not during the initial assault but during the attempts to secure and consolidate the new forward positions won.

Nevertheless, the British now had much improved observation over the area east of the Pilckem Ridge and from the Messines Ridge. It was now far safer for soldiers to move within The Salient in daylight hours. Moreover, the two sides had now arrived at a stalemate in the hollow between Pilckem and

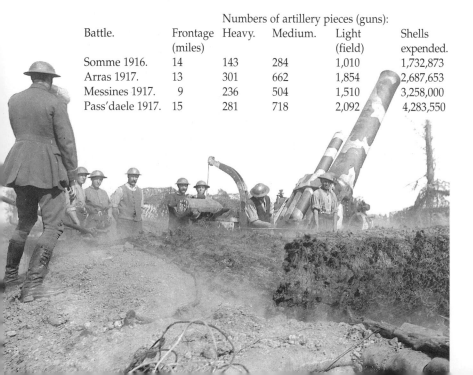

British Bunkers. *(opposite)*
The cluster of seven bunkers at Lankhof Farm, south of Ypres, are perhaps the best known, certainly the best preserved, of the Great War's grimly functional pieces of battlefield architecture. The bunkers were formed of concrete under corrugated iron whose shape was retained when the concrete set. Such bunkers could be created overnight and camouflaged with a great depth of earth and refuse. Inside almost nothing to reveal their original purpose is left. Outside the weeds grow and cattle graze languidly. What is both remarkable and certain is that the Lankhof Farm bunkers will outlast us all. Their builders have provided one of the most remarkable and brutal backdrops to any Belgian agrarian landscape.

Poelcappelle. The British Army had advanced to only a fraction of its first day's objectives losing between 30 to 60% of their fighting strength. Half of the tanks had already been made 'hors de combat'. With a humourless lack of concern the weather now took a turn for the worse. Rain and its concomitant, the mud, began to seize the initiative. Even on the evening of 31 July

precipitation was so heavy that troops in forward shellholes on the Gheluvelt approaches reported that they were soon flooded with knee-high water. Near the Steenbeek River, which was more a substantial drainage channel than river, to the west of Langemarck, the position was even worse with men being forced to stand for hours on end waist-deep in the cold water and clinging

Germans captured during the fighting for Pilckem Ridge

Polygon Wood and the Buttes New British Cemetery.

This is an area of enduring fascination. Close by the Buttes New British Cemetery is the New Zealand Memorial to the Missing and the imposing 5th Australian Division Memorial. The Butte is an embankment created as part of the old Belgian Army rifle range which had been used in the mid 19th century. Throughout the war years the Butte was tunnelled beneath, which ever side was in occupation seeking to take full advantage of its sheltering slopes. Close by is the old Ypres Military Riding School – the Polygon – whose outline featured prominently in all the military maps of the Great War relating to this area. The location was retained by the British during the First Battle of Ypres, lost at the Second Battle in May 1915 and recaptured by the 5th Australian Division in late September 1917.

As at Gallipoli you are as likely to meet an antipodean as a Lancastrian or Scotish traveller here. The cemetery contains graves from all periods of the Ypres fighting and has become the last resting place of soldiers from almost corner of the globe. When the sun is high enough to clear the trees which press close to the cemetery's boundaries the architecture and imposing height of the Butte topped by the Australian sunburst memorial can make an unforgettable sight.

mud which filled the lower reaches of their trenches.

Ten days after the start of the campaign, following a period of wet and stormy weather, a major attempt to break the deadlock was made at Westhoek, east of Ypres, and Glencorse Wood was captured by the British. Unfortunately such an advance could not disguise the fact that the Gheluvelt plateau was still securely in German hands. A week later another attack brought the British Army some success east of the Steenbeek when Langemarck village was captured.

This is perhaps the moment to introduce a vivid perspective of the fighting at this stage of the battle. It was written by Edwin Campion Vaughan, a young officer in 1917. This is a slightly abridged extract from his entry of 16 August, revealing by first-hand experience the impersonal impact of artillery fire and the scant regard which soldiers had for the comparably trivial issue of the bullet.

'August 16.....We were at Bridge 2A of the Yser canal, a few hundred yards north of Ypres. The air was poisoned by a terrible stench that turned me sick. In the dim light the water appeared to be a dark-green swamp wherein lay corpses of men and bodies of horses; shafts of waggons and gun wheels protruded from the putrefying mass and after a shuddering glance I hurried along the towing path to clearer air. The bank was honeycombed with dugouts, chiefly occupied by REs. At one point I saw a fingerboard "To the RC Chaplain"...Then, as the sky grew light, I walked along the path to where Sergeant Major Chalk was standing on the bank, silhouetted against the sky. I climbed up beside him and stood gazing across the darkness of the earth into the dawn. After a few minutes of silence he said "what is the time, Sir?"

"Four forty-five" I said, and with my words the whole earth burst into flame with one tremendous roar as hundreds of guns hurled the first round of the barrage. An instant's pause, then far in the distance we saw the faint line of fire where the shells were falling. Now the guns began crashing and pounding, keeping the air alive with shells screaming in different keys while the line of fire crackled unbrokenly in the distance. Spellbound I saw a line of coloured lights shoot up from the Boche and then Chalk tugged my sleeve to indicate that our Company was lining up on the towing path.

Scrambling down I slipped on my equipment as I ran forward to fall in beside Ewing. Then in file we moved forward through a gap in

Passchendaele village. (below and opposite)
Urbane and lofty in its outward appearance, Passchendaele has never sought to profit from its assured place in notoriety, even though many thousands of visitors pass through each year. There are no signs of welcome and few encouragements to parties or individuals to stop. Those shops and cafes which serve the area seem indifferent to the passage of so many travellers within and through the broad streets.

In winter this place is possessed of a forbidding climate. The buildings reflect that fact. Their roofs are steeply gabled, their brickwork solid, their windows shuttered against the elements. By 6.00 pm on a December evening the houses seem utterly devoid of life. Only in summer does Passchendaele acquire a human warmth as its fields and lanes hum with incessant agricultural activity. The spectre of what happened here still clearly stalks the conscience of Belgium, making people here reserved and wary of approach from outsiders.

The centre is impeccably restored. The cobbles and stonework are a testimony to the villagers' desire for permanence. The church and town hall are unadorned with ornament or frivolity. Here you will find few pointers to the past; a memorial plaque, a window in the church recording the part played by 66th (West Lancashire) Division. Standing here a while it is difficult to conjure up a mental image of what this place had become in November of 1917. A reddish stain in a sea of shell-holes, each filled with a noxious watery effluent. Rather tellingly the high ground of the Passchendaele ridge would soon be lost by the British Army during the German spring and early summer offensives of 1918. This is a place where the loneliness and human frailty which is part of every war is revealed to all who come. It is not a place to dwell within for long.

the bank on to a trench-board track. My nervousness was gone now; trembling with excitement, but outwardly perfectly reasonable, I drank in every detail of the scene almost with eagerness. To the east we moved along the winding track between batteries of heavies that belched smoke and fire as we passed. The light grew rapidly, and the line of fire changed to a line of smoke. Around us and ahead of us was earth, nothing but earth – no houses or trees or even grass – just faint shapeless humps from which the great guns hurled their iron death.

I was astounded that there was no retaliation; not a shell fell near us until we reached a sleeper track which Ewing told me was Buff's Road. Here we formed up in fours and marched on and on, the troops now singing lustily until I began to distinguish a different kind of crack and looking up I saw the horrible black curls of heavy shrapnel. These shook me a bit, but none came very near, and we approached closer and closer to the barrage that was now hidden from our sight by a slight ridge. The road had now almost disappeared and we were marching over shell-holes around which was scattered debris and wreckage at which I now dared not look. I kept my eyes fixed on the distance until we came to some low buildings – Van Heule Farm.

These were some of the concrete pillboxes of which we had heard. In front of them were six dead Germans and a disembowelled mule. Then I saw Colonel Hanson and Hoskins standing against the wall signalling to Ewing, who ran across to them. When he returned he led us off the road to the right, on to the churned stretch of shell-holes, and gave the signal for artillery formation. I led my platoon off to the right and we continued to move steadily across that muddy waste until I realised that we were walking into a curtain of fire. We were right on top of the German barrage when glancing round I saw Ewing give the signal to halt.

I repeated the signal to my men, and we all dived into shell-holes right on the fringe of the shell-torn zone. With my head just over the edge of my shell-hole I lay blinking into the shrieking, crashing hail of death 30 yards in front. We were too close to fear anything except a direct hit and fascinated I stared at that terrible curtain through which we soon must pass. One gun was firing regularly onto a spot only a few yards in front of me and as I watched the bursts I became aware of Private Bishop in the shell-hole in front with a thick red stream running down his back. I shouted to him, 'Are you hurt,

Bishop?' Turning round he said, 'No, Sir' in surprise. So I leaped across the edge of the hole and found that the stream proceeded from a shrapnel wound in a carton of jam in his haversack.

We were laughing about this when a runner tumbled in on us – for now machine gun bullets were sweeping over us – and told me that Ewing wanted me to send a patrol to find Border House which, when located, I was to occupy. I sent Corporal Wood on this job, and having watched him disappear into the barrage, I sat down to await his return. It only seemed a few minutes before he returned, saying he had found it, but one man had been killed.

Dully I hoisted myself out of the mud and gave the signal to advance, which was answered by every man rising and stepping unhesitatingly into the barrage. The effect was so striking that I felt no more that awful dread of the shellfire, but followed them calmly into the crashing, spitting hell until we were surrounded by bursting shells and singing fragments, while above us a stream of bullets added their whining to the general pandemonium. The men were wonderful! And it was astounding that although no one ran or ducked, whilst many were blown over by shells bursting at our very feet no one was touched until we were through the thickest part of the barrage and making for the little ridge in front.

Then I saw fellows drop lifeless while others began to stagger and limp; the fragments were getting us and in front was a belt of wire. At this moment I felt my feet sink and though I struggled to get on, I was dragged down to the waist in sticky clay. The others passed on, not noticing my plight until by yelling and firing my revolver into the air I attracted the attention of Sergeant Gunn, who returned and dragged me out. I caught up the troops who were passing through a gap in the wire, and I was following Corporal Breeze when a shell burst at his feet. As I was blown backwards I saw him thrown into the air to land at my feet, a crumpled heap of torn flesh.

Sick with horror I scrambled over him and stumbled down into the cutting, which was the Steenbeck [sic] Stream. Crouched in here we found the Irish Rifles, and we lined up with them. There was a padre who gave me a cheery grin and further along was a major smoking a pipe as he sat on the bank with his back to the enemy. I climbed out of the stream and saluted him, noticing out of the corner

(Opposite) The slopes below Passchendaele at Zonnebeke were stripped of foliage and features. Shattered trees and scattered pill boxes became the only landmarks on the barren landscape.

of my eye that a tank was ditched in the cutting. I sat down beside him and told him who we were, and then from the heap of flesh that had been Breeze, I saw the stump of an arm raised an inch or two. Others saw it too and before I needed to tell them, the stretcher-bearers were on their way to him. Very gently they brought him in to where I was sitting. He was terribly mutilated, both his feet had gone and one arm, his legs and trunk were torn to ribbons and his face was dreadful. But he was conscious and as I bent over him I saw in his remaining eye a gleam of mingled recognition and terror. His feeble hand clutched my equipment, and then the light faded from his eye. The shells continued to pour but we gave poor Breezy a burial in a shell-hole and the padre read a hurried prayer.'

[Source: E.C.Vaughan. *Some Desperate Glory*. Pen & Sword Books.]

Shells burst on Pilckem Ridge as soldiers watch during the battle for Langemarck.

(Opposite) During the battle of the Menin Road Ridge men of the 13th Durham Light Infantry wait to go over the top on 20 September. The anxiety is palpable – no cheery glances to the photographer from these tense and frightened soldiers who reveal the stress of battle in all their mannerisms.

On 27 August the British managed to push forwards more than a mile along the St. Julien to Poelcappelle road, south-east of Langemarck. The pattern of separate assaults within an intent to seek the higher ground was already established.

By 15 September the British were able to launch the Second Phase of the battle with a series of closely staged attacks. Within five days that phase was broadened into the massive assaults known collectively as the Battle of Menin Road - in reality an enormous effort across a wide frontage undertaken by both the Second and Fifth Armies, from Zillebeke in the south of The Salient to Langemarck in the north. At the close of these events the Australians had captured the western portion of the notorious Polygon Wood, between the villages of Gheluvelt, on the Menin Road, and Zonnebeke below

Passchendaele. Six days later, on 26 September, the battle for Zonnebeke and Polygon Wood began. The fighting within the splintered remains of the wood was of a most intense and brutal magnitude.

North of Polygon Wood much of the village of Zonnebeke also fell, although by now the conditions which the troops were enduring were alien to all previous human experience. The British Army was paying the price for its wanton destruction of the area's drainage system. The water simply had nowhere to go. It slewed out of the numerous shattered stream courses in broad swathes of loathsomely smelling, glutinously adhesive slime.

Throughout these periods of unremitting conflict German troops contested every assault. Sometimes the counter-attacks were of a localised nature, but that which took place on 1 October, at Zonnebeke, Polygon Wood and near to the Menin Road, shook the British troops with its ferocity and intent. It was very clear that the German Army was no spent force at this stage.

It is interesting to compare the style of Edwin Vaughan's account with the practised understatement of battle-hardened brigade staff. Each battalion within a brigade had an adjutant whose role it was to deal with the battalion's administration and record-keeping. His reports of actions would

(Opposite) Germans captured at Broodseinde. Their faces reveal a mixture of defiance, relief, exhaustion and stress. The youthfulness of many is apparent. By 1918 both sides would be freely employing eighteen-year-old soldiers to fill the gaps in every rank.

subsequently be condensed by Brigade staff to form reports to be passed on to divisional, corps and army command. Here the 22nd Brigade summarise the German counter-attacks on some of the 7th Division's troops (Manchester Pals), in the Polygon Wood area that day.

'After about an hour's intense bombardment the enemy came over in three waves, attacking across the whole of the brigade front...The first wave just succeeded in reaching our trenches, but was wiped out by rifle and Machine Gun Fire. Of the 2nd and 3rd waves, those who did not become casualties from barrage or our rifle fire, ran back to

Passchendaele Ridge *(below)*
This is the view of the ridge which the hapless British soldiers had as they waded waist deep in the sea of mud which had gathered in the bowl below the ridge. Many were to end up in the cemetery at Tyne Cot which now occupies the crest.

their rear...Lieutenant Colonel Turnbull, 20th Manchester Regiment, when in the front line of trenches, directing operations of his battalion, was unfortunately killed...For some few hours no further attack took place, but the intense barrage was continued on our front and support trenches and to a great depth in the back areas...Two Machine Guns having been put out of action by shell fire, two more were ordered up from the Reserve Section at Zillebeke Lake. The sergeant conducting these and the carrying party were either wounded or killed and the guns destroyed. Two more guns were therefore sent up to replace them.' [Public Record Office. WO/95 1661.]

On 4 October both sides planned attacks to the east of Ypres. That launched by the British anticipated their opponents' intent by just a few minutes. As a result the Tommies and their ANZAC comrades pushed forward into Poelcappelle and past the two hamlets of Gravenstafel and Broodseinde below Passchendaele. Thus, at the end of the Battle of Broodseinde, fought for in the most terrible and inclement weather amidst deep clinging mud, the British Army was 9,000 yards from the Menin Gate and 2,200 yards from the centre of Passchendaele village. Since 31 July they had advanced 6,000 yards. By any means of assessing the cost it was clear that casualties were heavy. However, an even sterner test of resolve was still to come.

The second week in October 1917 marked the start of the third phase of the Third Battle of Ypres. Principally this took the form of attacks in a north-easterly direction towards Houthulst Forest on the north of The Salient. However, in the context of the battle for Passchendaele these assaults need not deflect our attention. The final battle for Passchendaele was about to be engaged.

This unenviable task would be given to the Australians, New Zealanders and Canadians.

The Canadian Memorial at Passchendaele. (opposite)
Canadian soldiers left their imprint on all significant theatres of the Western Front. Their memorials are characterised by an economy and simplicity which does away, at a stroke, with the idea that war is glorious. Perhaps the most significant of these simple granite structures is this, here below Passchendaele village. It marks the site of Crest Farm, reached by the Canadian infantry on 30 October 1917.

It would be intolerable to complete this account of the Third Battle of Ypres without giving due prominence to the role played by these redoubtable Empire soldiers. To look today at the long lines of headstones within Tyne Cot cemetery, all too often bearing the Maple Leaf or Sun Burst insignia of a Canadian or Australian regiment, is to know just a fragment of what was given here. Put simply, the Empire soldiers were the backbone of the British Army's attempts to fight their way onto the highest ground of the Passchendaele ridge. In those final weeks as the conflict edged its way towards that summit it was these Australians, the New Zealanders and ultimately the Canadians whose resilience triumphed.

On 12 October the First Battle for Passchendaele was fought. Rain and mud had now seriously compromised the ability of all combatants to move. To maintain a functional rifle in the filth generated by a major artillery bombardment and subsequent infantry assault was almost impossible. The few tracks across the wasteland below Passchendaele ridge were the predictable target of German artillery. Away from those tracks, which the pioneers and engineers tried desperately to maintain, the waterlogged shellholes interlocked, creating conditions in which men who slipped from the narrow edges into the sucking slime below were sometimes unable to free themselves. This was the unforgettable hell that was the Battle for

Passchendaele. Eighty years later the mere thought of this was sufficient to reduce its participants to tears and shock.

A fortnight later the Second Battle for Passchendaele was engaged, this time with the Canadian Corps in the forefront. Incremental moves edged the troops forward amidst the most inhuman conditions and intense defence. Passchendaele was by now nothing more than a stain on the landscape. Every vestige of structure was literally blown off the summit as artillery pulverised the positions without let up. By 30 October the Canadians were fighting in the outskirts of the village.

A week later it was all but over.

As the sun rose on the morning of 6 November, unseen behind a curtain of malevolent shellbursts and leaden skies, the final assault upon the village of Passchendaele was launched. It fell to soldiers who found nothing there. There was nothing. There wasn't even a German counter-attack. It was as if the brutal truth of what had happened here had numbed each and every participant. Those who had survived had seen the very worst that humanity had fashioned in the name of war. It had been the most degrading event in the history of man. However, it had not been the most costly. That dubious privilege was retained, at this early stage in the twentieth century's extraordinary history, by the 1916 Somme campaign.

British Army casualties during the Third Battle of Ypres were calculated as

Stretcher bearers listen sympathetically to a seriously wounded soldier. One man records the soldier's words – perhaps a last letter to someone at home.

244,897. Of course a very considerable proportion of those wounded, within the above figure, were later returned to duty. The losses to the German Army have long been the subject of debate around the issue of whether, in the attritional sense, it had all been worthwhile. The likelihood is that the German Army lost 400,000 men during the fighting east of Ypres during the autumn of 1917. More than 35,000 British soldiers, both officers and other ranks, were known to be dead. The missing amounted to almost 30,000 further souls.

Tyne Cot. *(opposite)*

For most visitors this place defines the battles for Passchendaele village. The cemetery is located short of the crest of Passchendaele Ridge below the final approaches to the village from the west. Tyne Cot and its remarkable architecture was thus, during the last weeks of the battle, epicentral in the most intense of that fighting.

If you stand upon the lowest step of the Cross of Sacrifice you will see the panoply of the Third Battle of Ypres spread in front. On a clear day the spire of St.Martin's Cathedral and the Cloth Hall's tower are clearly visible in the midst of distant Ypres. Sometimes they seem suspended in haze which shrouds the surrounding and lesser buildings. That view tells, with impeccable clarity, the history of the Battle for Passchendaele.

Within the symmetry of the cemetery lies an incredible weight of detail. It is the largest Commonwealth War Graves Commission cemetery with over 11,900 graves. The greatest swathe of burials are those of men killed during 1917 and subsequently found during battlefield clearances - the grim task which went on unabated until the early 1930s. No less than seventy per cent of the bodies buried here are unidentified. Most of the cemetery is, therefore, a concentration of bodies found after the war. The original battlefield cemetery, just behind the Cross of Sacrifice, is an irregular grouping of 350 graves in the haphazard form of the first hasty burials. A number of these graves hold many men, hurriedly tumbled into pits containing four, eight or even a dozen men's shell torn remains. The cemetery's design has incorporated three massive German bunkers, a ubiquitous feature of the 1917 battlefields.

The Memorial to the Missing. At the back of the cemetery, forming its eastern wall, are the ranks of the missing. Each panel records those soldiers from many regiments of the Empire and British forces whose bodies were never recovered from the battlefield after the Passchendaele campaign. The decision to commemorate these 35,000 souls stems from an arbitrary date, 15 August 1917, after which the missing were destined to be recorded here, before then upon the Menin Gate. Unlike the towering Thiepval memorial this is a subdued and accessible place. Discreetly placed, behind the memorial panels, are small enclosed lawn gardens where bereaved families wept in less public grief when they came here in their thousands during the 1930s. The place is no less frequently visited today although those visitors are now as likely to be fifth generation descendants, the curious, the students of war, school children, organised parties or the local community whose members share the quiet dignity of this deeply impressive place with its many visitors.

Many amongst that terrible statistic had been swept away by shellfire, their ravaged remains sunk within the putrid mud which was the essence of this battlefield. Others had simply drowned, unable to save themselves under the weight of equipment or the debilitating effects of wounds or exhaustion.

The myth of the mud as winner.

Mud is one of the most lingering popular images of the Great War. At Passchendaele by late October the mire was certainly widespread. Its principal source was the numerous shell holes which in heavily contested locations on the battlefield were so adjacent that there was little room between each hole for a man to stand upon. In periods of unremitting wet weather every crater became a potential trap for the unwary. However, we should not slip into the pitfall of believing that mud was both the winner and the only defining feature of this campaign.

The Official History of the Passchendaele fighting was published in 1948 - three years after the Second World War's end. It is a measure of the task's magnitude that the 'Official' history of that first great twentieth century conflict should not have been concluded before the next cataclysmic world struggle had subsided. However, the passage of time gave the historian time to reflect upon the extent of the mud at Third Ypres and to place that issue in context. One senior officer commanding the engineering branch of the 56th

After the battle for Passchendaele Canadian Pioneers undertake the terrible process of battlefield clearance, putting the remains of soldiers into sandbags for burial and collecting equipment for refurbishment.

The Cross of Sacrifice. (opposite)
This is the most symbolic landmark upon all the Great War's numerous battlefields. Here at Tyne Cot the Portland stone structure is built above a German command bunker whose grey concrete was employed to elevate the cross into its present position. Each British cemetery is graced by one of these crosses which seem to pick up and resonate sunlight in a way which invariably attracts the eye's attention. Inlaid into each cross is a symbolic bronze sword upon which so much life was sacrificed and which is now defeated by the power of reconciliation, peace and love.

Division was recorded as saying that:

'Some accounts of the Passchendaele campaign leave the impression that it rained continuously for weeks and months, and that the terrain was a morass. This was not my experience. I have been wetter and muddier on the Somme in 1916, October especially. What is true, I think, is that around Ypres the shell holes were more numerous to the acre than on the Somme.'

Many other testimonies are used to support the contention that underfoot conditions towards the end of the Somme campaign, especially during the Battle of the Ancre, were worse than those here at Passchendaele. That conclusion is almost certainly true but the November Battle of the Ancre in 1916 was a confined event within a narrow valley location. Beneath Passchendaele the extent of the waterlogged, shell-swept and contested zone was more extensive and utterly devoid of features. From the muddy shellholes and swamp-like slit trenches which the fighting men inhabited

every vista confirmed their small and menacing world to be a sea of mud. But it was the same for soldiers of both contesting sides whose combat troops fought within this eerily inhospitable and waterlogged terrain. For all front line troops the conditions during the last weeks of Third Ypres in the contested zones were physically demanding and immensely stressful. The judgement on the British side was that Tommy was in a better position to bear that strain than his German counterpart, and that it was therefore worthwhile prolonging the campaign beyond the serious deterioration in the weather of early October.

These terrible conditions were being wrought by artillery and the monstrous agglomeration of munitions into a confined battlefield area. Every small incremental advance had to be made across shell-torn ground. Last month's front line positions became this week's rear areas across which supplies had to be moved. Understandably the effects of preceding heavy barrages on the topography made the artillery's work increasingly problematic, more so than any former experience could have suggested. One senior officer from the Royal Artillery commented that:

> '....since early October Napoleon's 'fifth element' - mud - had become a factor of the gravest importance. Even August had been unusually wet, and since then the ground, always waterlogged and now thoroughly cut up, had steadily got worse and worse. The mere movement of artillery and supply of ammunition under peace [time] conditions would have been a Herculean task; it was scarcely possible to walk off the duckboards. All ammunition supply to the more advanced batteries was perforce carried out by packing, mules were constantly engulfed, and even guns in considerable numbers were swallowed up in the sea of mud.'

At first sight this artilleryman's view seems to be in contradiction with the interpretation made by the 56th Division's engineers. In reality he is simply stating the obvious. Of course conditions were very difficult, especially when heavy guns had to be moved and infantry had to occupy ground from which

Talbot House at 'Pop'. *(opposite)*

It is a popular misconception that men involved in the Great War spent months on end in trenches. Soldiers had to be given relief. From the forward front line trenches companies of men would move back into support and reserve positions to be replaced by another company from the same battalion. Scattered in nearby farm cellars would be signallers, advanced company headquarters and carrying parties. Supervising, perhaps a mile to the rear, would be the battalion's commanding officer and second in command, as well as the adjutant and medical officer. Their dug-outs were a prime target for artillery which constantly sought to disrupt command and

communication. The rotation would continue for some days before the battalion was taken out of the lines altogether.

Whether in support or out of the lines the men's time was always taken with fatigues, carrying parties, construction work and endless training. Sometimes a battalion within its brigade or division would find itself on the move to another sector where battle was anticipated, or billeted to the rear whilst their division was supplemented with new drafts of men. The replacement of men lost to the ideals of attrition was essential after major set-piece battles. The return of an exhausted unit to the rear for refitting, as it was anodynely known, would be a trying time for the survivors.

During the war's first three years the small town of Poperinghe was far enough west of Ypres to be relatively safe from shelling and aerial attack. In 1917 air raids by Gotha bombers became more frequent but the town stood firm. Many civilians stayed throughout and watched as the station funnelled hundreds of thousands of soldiers through; the wounded on ambulance trains, those going on leave, those returning and the units in transit. The trucks bore an ubiquitous legend 'Hommes 40 - Chevaux 10' chalked on the side. Troops were billeted in vast numbers. Estaminets served a steady diet of eggs, cheap beers and wines, bread and fried foods to the men. Junior officers frequented the cafes and restaurants and were plied with marginally better fare when they could afford it. Those with the money and inclination could use the brothels which were tolerated by the military authorities - both here and in other towns behind the lines in France such as Armentières, one of whose mademoiselles was made famous by a racy song, extemporised upon endlessly by a thousand thousand men. The brothels were brutal and appalling places where the trade in sex was completely dehumanised.

Pop or Pops, as the troops affectionately called this place, was no place for the weak or infirm. It was a hive of activity. Feeding, watering, bathing and delousing were its central functions for ordinary Tommy. Factories and houses alike were commandeered by higher military authority for use as administrative facilities, command centres, communications centres and stores for vast arrays of materiel. Railways brought hundreds of tons of supplies and thousands of men here on a daily basis. Ambulances and medical evacuations were in evidence everywhere.

Yet in the centre of this hubble of activity was Talbot House. It was the inspiration of two men, the Reverend Philip Bayard 'Tubby' Clayton and the Reverend Neville Talbot. The unassuming town house was acquired in 1915 and became a beacon of humanity and dignity. A notice at the door enjoined all who passed through to 'abandon rank all ye who enter'. Fraternity and the opportunity to write letters, view films, read in peace and quiet, and attend services, held in the hop loft above which had been converted into a chapel, drew men of all denominations and backgrounds here.

The history of Talbot House and its place in the subsequent establishment of the Toc-H organisation is utterly inspirational. More completely than any other place, any museum or display this location encompasses the spirit of the period and the sense of hope which inspired all who sought solace here from the despair, devastation and depravity which they had come to know as war. To come to this place, at the very end of the twentieth century, is to be calmed.

all vestiges of shelter had been torn away by shellfire. Nevertheless, the infantry, gunners and logisticians were prepared and able to cope with these hugely difficult circumstances in order to achieve a desired outcome. Today such willing sacrifice is almost impossible to visualise or understand at such distance. In the end it was the physical wear upon the artillery and the casualties amongst the specialist gunnery teams which ensured, more effectively than the prevalence of mud, that the campaign had to be ended. Put simply, it was plain to Haig that were the campaign not to end there would be no serviceable British artillery available for a spring offensive in 1918. The incidental capture of Passchendaele had little if any strategic significance in November of 1917 and, in its own right, had little to do with the decision to abort the campaign after its fall.

As events transpired it was the German army which launched the first

The deployment of tanks often resulted in mechanical failure. The open terrain criss crossed with ditches, trenches and water courses meant that many machines became bogged down and easy prey to the German artillery.

spring offensive the following year. That offensive was a gambler's final throw of the dice in a last-ditch attempt to win the war with one colossal and conclusive blow. The eventual failure of that offensive was rooted in the impact of the British campaign in Flanders during the final months of 1917. A stunning success could have been won by Germany had it not been for the depletion of their best divisions in Belgium and the overfacing of their artillery and air force units by the resilient determination of the British armed forces during 1917. By the onset of winter German reserves were reduced to a level of virtual elimination with the consequence that sick, unrecovered and under-age men of 18 were 'thrust into both the war-hardened divisions already in France and into the less experienced and less sternly disciplined divisions brought to France from the Russian front.' What was, therefore, clearly the most conclusive outcome of the battle for Passchendaele from the British perspective was that it had been fought and that a long-term advantage had been won. By sheer willpower and unimaginable human endeavour the British Army made the battle for this unremarkable plot of land into an issue which shattered German resolve and reserves.

Once again the German psyche had allowed his armed forces to be drawn into a battle of attrition. It was an utterly futile, crucial and ultimately war-losing error of strategy.

END STOP...

There can be no conclusion to a book such as this. There is no end to the history and interpretation of the Great War. It was, and remains, one of the most significant events in man's recent and chequered history. The consequences of the war and its settlement at Versailles are still being felt today. In many respects the Great War was itself the begetter of what subsequent generations came to know as the Second World War. Many cemeteries upon the Somme and within The Salient have been widened in scope to accept the more recent arrivals of men killed during the fighting which spilled blood on those same soils, just twenty years after the end of the Great War.

As I write these closing words preparations are in hand for the funeral service of one Joe Fitzpatrick – a man possessed of the most lucid and retentive memory of the Great War, one of the best that I ever met. Joe died aged 103. These coming years will also mark the extinction of a final dwindling band of men and women who also knew the war. A tiny group of resilient participants, born in the late 19th century, will eventually be able to say that their lives have spanned three centuries. It was a great privilege to have known a little of their part in these terrible events. Yet they were nothing new in the history of man's conflicts. Fighting attracts the brave and the honourable, yet it also draws inexorably upon the dishonourable, the cowardly, the hesitant and those who simply never wanted to be there. To imagine that the Great War was fought entirely by the finest men which Victorian and Edwardian Britain had made is demonstrable nonsense. In his seemingly youthful nineties Joe was always prepared to remind me of that. Many things were done in the name of war which men were later ashamed of. Some men proved wilfully capable of behaving in a cowardly and shameful manner. Prisoners were ill-treated, sometimes killed in the terror and confusion of battle. Civilian populations were ousted from their homes and history in the search for accommodation for weary fighting men. Property was appropriated and stolen with little regard for propriety and the rights of ownership. Many ill-considered attacks paid too little attention to the suffering which would be consequential upon those decisions to advance.

But aside from the isolated examples of the worst there were ubiquitous examples of the highest and finest standards of behaviour. Officers led with selfless disregard and enormous bravery. Fortitude amongst all was commonplace. Bravery was expected of the common soldier, and often went unremarked. The spirit of sharing and the love of others who shared danger and privation was the norm of soldierly behaviour and respect. Millions at home bore terrible apprehension and foreboding with equanimity and courage. The numbers of widows and companionless women created by the war were legion. These women often lived lives utterly bereft of human compensation – yet their dignity in so doing was unending.

There are clear lessons for us contained within the story of the Great War. Comradeship, team work and determination are the human and managerial qualities which breed successful outcomes to complex issues. You might have thought it sensible to include the word 'planning', but the Great War is studded with so many examples of the way in which the best laid plans were quickly compromised, and therefore rendered a distraction, by events that are too numerous to mention. Perhaps it is worth saying that making plans at the outset about how you will fight an impending war often turns into an imperative course which you are obliged to follow with enormously costly consequences.

The morality of the Great War is so often debated and yet never defined. The concept of the sanctity of human life sits ill at ease with the attrition of the years between 1916 and the end of the war. Within the killing fields of the western front men would learn the value of life, yet willingly sacrifice their

own in the attempt to save others. The churches have wrestled for centuries with the abstraction of a just war. The Second World War is often referred to as a just, almost moral, war, the fighting of which was necessary to combat evil. By contrast the Great War seems to many to have been utterly without moral purpose, its outbreak the consequence of self-seeking political imperatives. Yet the church played an active role in the dissemination of propaganda and the recruitment of personnel for the armed forces of all major European belligerents. In that context many pacifists have come to view participation in war as morally repugnant because its killing has little to do with morality and all to do with the politics of nationality, ethnicity, self-righteous indignation or greed.

The most accessible way into this extraordinary history is to visit these remarkable places where the war was fought. Travel to France and Belgium is inexpensive. Gallipoli is more problematic but increasingly accessible. The rewards of insight and immense pleasure at the knowledge gained are huge. I would be less than truthful if I did not say that the places identified within this book can move visitors' emotions freely. Perhaps one appropriate measure of the success of this television series and book will be if many of you, for the first time, subsequently launch forth into the extraordinary world of the Great War's history.

Nowhere is that history more rewarding, challenging and inspirational than on the ground. It has been said before and it merits saying again now. If you haven't been yet to some or all of these places, I can only counsel that you should. No life would seem to me complete without the impact and insight which such a visit will certainly bring. One word of warning though. I know almost no-one who has been just once. These places have the power to draw you back again and again.

To help and support visitors to these unique locations at the very heart of twentieth century history the publishers of this work are also responsible for innovative and immensely informative guidebooks in the *Battleground Europe* series. The telephone number at the front of this book will bring you details. Within that sequence of books are more than twenty volumes covering, in minute detail, the locations and events portrayed in images here. From those texts, all written by acknowledged authorities in each battle and location, you can get precise details of how to travel, where to stay, and how to tour and walk these places as if guided by your own personal and always attentive escort. The books are written in an accessible style making first time visits approachable with confidence, yet with sufficient detail to inform the expert and regular traveller alike. I hope to see you there.